5.8

WOMEN
WOMEN
WOMEN

Quips, Quotes, and Commentary

WOMEN
WOMEN
WOMEN

Quips, Quotes, and Commentary

Leta W. Clark

DRAKE PUBLISHERS INC · NEW YORK · LONDON

Published in 1977 by
Drake Publishers, Inc.
801 Second Avenue
New York, N.Y. 10017

Library of Congress Cataloging in Publication Data
Main entry under title:

Women, women, women.

   1. Women—Quotations.   2. Women—Quotations,
maxims, etc. I. Clark, Leta W.
HQ1399.W64   082   77-6927
ISBN 0-8473-1612-2
ISBN 0-8473-1586-X pbk.

Design: Harold Franklin

Printed in the United States of America

CONTENTS

List of Illustrations

Photo Credits

WOMEN
WOMEN
WOMEN
Quips, Quotes, and Commentary

The first thing I discovered when I began researching this book was that in the past nobody seems to have written down what women said. Going through the books of quotations was rather like strolling through the major art museums. There are millions of paintings, all done by men. Obviously there were women out there someplace, painting and sculpting — and receiving no recognition.

During the past ten years, there has been increased emphasis on unearthing the output of women in all areas. This book, which locates and assembles the words of women, is part of that quest.

As I began to gather material, the chapter divisions became self-evident. These were the areas of life that were and are important to us. Within each category opinions and attitudes differed as to focus, but were similar in intensity. If I am permitted one generalization, it would be that women tend to internalize. They speak from their whole beings, not just their minds.

There have been many people who have helped me with this book. Gratitude is a mild word for what I feel toward Ted Gottfried, the editor who thought up the idea. He did not waver in his conviction that there are enough important words by women to make a book, and there are enough human beings interested in these words to make up a book audience.

My thanks to Patrice LoCicero for her enthusiastic help, to Bill Simons for his clarity and support, and to my women friends for their optimism, their assurances — and their words.

Leta W. Clark
June 6, 1977

Chapter One:

WHAT WOMEN SAY ABOUT THEMSELVES

To me, one of the special delights in listening to women talk
about themselves is their sense of irreverence. Nothing is sacred;
the masks are pulled off, the myths debunked. Their words
seem couched in a sense of physical self that is brave, optimistic,
pragmatic, and comically honest. They are what they are:
the beginning, the end, everything, and nothing.

I'm sure there are many rationales for this irreverence.
Since women have been outside the system for so many centuries,
it would be odd if they had not worked out an inner language
that permitted them to puncture the pomposities.

There is a "grounded-ness" in their conversation. Listen
to some of them . . .

*Now I am beginning to live a little and feel less like a sick oyster
at low tide.*

> Louisa May Alcott, 1832 - 1888
> Journal

I've been Goddamned lucky. I've had a pretty fascinating life.

> Katharine Hepburn
> People, October 11, 1976

When she was an ambassador, Shirley Temple Black spoke
of the difficulties of diplomatic life:

> *If you're in a situation different from anything you've
> been through before, you just have to stand up straight
> and forge ahead.*
>
> *. . . I have been fortunate, because the name
> Shirley Temple opens many doors. But if you don't have
> something to contribute, the doors can close very rapidly.*

> People, September 13, 1976

*I seldom think about my limitations, and they never make me sad.
Perhaps there is just a touch of yearning at times; but it is vague,
like a breeze among flowers.*

> Helen Keller

In her book, *Widow*, Lynn Caine explored the emotional
transition from wife to widow. She summarizes a portion
of that transition:

> *Gradually I learned that surviving pessimism was not
> living. Yet for me, as for many, it was a comfortable place to be,
> a neutral place. Much harder, in a way, was learning to go beyond
> mere survival to find the courage to build and to grow and
> especially to build and grow by myself.*

> Vogue, January, 1975

Shirley Temple Black

*It's stupid to describe me as hard. I'm the most sensitive
creature you'll ever meet. It's no accident many accuse me
of conducting public affairs with my heart instead of my head.
Well, what if I do? I see no harm in it, on the contrary.
I've always felt sorry for people afraid of feeling, of sentimen-
tality, of emotion, who conceal what they feel and are unable
to weep with their whole heart. Because those who do not
know how to weep with their whole heart don't know how
to laugh either.*

Golda Meir
Oriana Fallaci, MS, April, 1973

*I'm writing this by the window in the music room on a little
table, after the children have gone to bed. A large school, a staff,
overflowing infant room and three children of our own at home
. . . the need for regular breaths of silence, the wetting of the
lips, mouth and throat with the water of silence, is more desperate
than before. What about my music, my thinking, my study
and my attempt at writing, and the drawing which I loved? What
hope of survival for that area within that is the real me? Denying
all that, how can I remain sufficiently whole to become a worthwhile person. A worthwhile person must be* all *there.*

*There's only one thing to do, o my self. Make yourself a
place. The hills are very much too far away to use for a cave
and to get there is a mile's walk in full view. I don't like such a
distance from home and I never liked "full view." Besides, something these days is moving me to settle nearer home; whatever
I make for myself will be closer than the whare or the cave,
closer again to home.*

Sylvia Ashton-Warner
Myself, Simon & Schuster

*When people sometimes ask me, men occasionally, "don't you
do anything?" — because I don't play tennis, I don't play golf,
I don't do needlepoint — I have that old feeling that, my God,
there's nothing that I can do.*

When I was young, I didn't feel that there was anything

really that I could do well. Maybe that's why I worked. In the
last few years I've realized that it isn't all luck, that I am good
at what I do. But I can count the number of things I can do
on one hand.

Barbara Walters
Vogue, June, 1975

Writer Joan Mills talks about her mid-life insights:
I'd gone through life believing in the strength and
competence of others; never in my own. Now, dazzled,
I discovered that my capacities were real. It was like
finding a fortune in the lining of an old coat.

Humility is not my forte, and whenever I dwell for any length
of time on my own shortcomings, they gradually begin to seem
mild, harmless, rather engaging little things, not at all like the
staring defects in other people's characters.

Margaret Halsey
With Malice Toward Some

Humorist and radio performer Jane Ace is quoted by her husband,
Goodman Ace, as describing herself:
I'm a ragged individualist.

I sometimes give myself admirable advice but I am incapable
of taking it.

Lady Mary Wortley Montagu, 1689 - 1762
English poet and letter writer

The quest for self-definition haunted Janis Joplin throughout
her career. A few years before her death she said:
When I first started singing I was copying Bessie Smith
records. I used to sing exactly like Bessie Smith, and when
I started singing with Big Brother that was the only thing

I knew how to do, and used to wonder — especially when
people would clap and tell me good — I used to wonder,
"Is that real or is that something I've learned to do with
my voice?" But I think after doing it for a few years I got
to understand that it all ties in. I used to ask guys I was
balling, "Do I ball like I sing? Is it really me?" That's what
I'm trying to say. It is really me, or am I putting on a show
. . . and that's what I wonder sometimes when I'm talking.
Is this person that's talking me? Does what I'm saying
correlate with my music?

David Dalton
Janis, 1971

An earlier performer had none of these self-doubts. Silent movie
queen Theda Bara (the Vamp) tantalized her public with state-
ments like:

The reason good women like me flock to my pictures is that
there is a little bit of vampire instinct in every woman.

In 1974, headlines from the West Coast told of the disappearance
and search for Angelina Alioto, the wife of a California political
figure. She reappeared after eighteen days, and made this
statement:

I love my husband very, very much, but he didn't ask me
when he ran for mayor and he didn't consult me about
running for governor. It would be nice to be asked.
. . . You know, I've been my mother's daughter, my
father's daughter, the wife of my husband, the mother of
my six children, and grandmother to my eleven grand-
children, but I have never been me. But I am now because
I went away. I am a changed woman.

Theda Bara

Rosa Bonheur

*I have no patience with women who ask permission to think.
Let women establish their claims by great and good work, and
not by conventions.*

>Rosa Bonheur
>French artist
>1841

Betty Friedan, speaking about her life following the publication
of *The Feminine Mystique:*

>*Personally, I couldn't operate as a suburban housewife
any longer, even if I had wanted to. For one thing, I became
a leper in my own suburb. As long as I only wrote occasional
articles most people never read, the fact that I wrote during
the hours when the children were in school was no more a
stigma than, for instance, solitary morning drinking. But now
that I was acting like a real writer and even being interviewed
on television, the sin was too public, it could not be condoned.
Women in other suburbs were writing me as if I were Joan of
Arc, but I practically had to flee my own crabgrass-overgrown
yard to keep from being burned at the stake. Although we
had been fairly popular, my husband and I were suddenly
no longer invited to our neighbors' dinner parties. My kids
were kicked out of the car pool for art and dancing classes
. . . we had to move back to the city . . . I couldn't stand
being a freak alone in the suburbs . . .*
>
>Betty Friedan, Epilogue, 1975, *The Feminine Mystique,*
>Dell Publishing

Barbara Howar, having been fired from her job by the Lyndon
Johnsons, described her reaction:

>*I was filled with an uncontrollable desire to shock — to say
or do anything that would raise voices and eyebrows or
boredom's threshold. I had a natural ability to alienate
people I found dull. I would rudely cut short any matron
lady who dwelled too long on her wonderful children, her
indispensable housekeeper, or her husband's unheralded
political abilities. I once interrupted a woman deep into*

*her monologue about the Great Lone Star State with, "If I
hear one more exaggeration about Texas I'm going to throw
up the Alamo." I became incautious in my description of
Texas habits, asking one gentleman sporting a hammered
silver belt studded with ersatz stones, "Did you make it
at summer camp?" And to a Dallas lady in reference to the
Tex-Mex delicacy she had proudly served for dinner, "Did
you get this recipe off the back of a Frito's bag?"*

Barbara Howar
Laughing All the Way

My vigor, vitality and cheek repel me. I am the kind of woman
I would run from.

Lady Nancy Astor
British political figure, 1930's

When I came into Macmillan Hall, my friend Sidney warned
there'd be trouble, the place full of radical lesbians wanting me
to clear things up, contradict the press image of nice married
lady. Straight. Okay. Someone from Time came when I talked
at Daughters of Bilitis, a lesbian group, in August, candid, one
gay to another. But they didn't pick it up. Chattered Gay Lib
politics with Barbara Love the whole day Life interviewed me.
The pregnant lady reporter seemed not to want the baby.
Didn't like me. Said I swore, printed fifteen curse words in
two columns. Misquoted me, saying lesbianism was "not my
bag." Printed a picture of me kissing Fumio. Saw it one night
in a bar when he was gone in Japan. Drunk and tired, shooting
the film ("Three Lives.") Wept, missing him. Mother will not
have to live with her neighbors reading the unspeakable. Mother
will not thunder at me . . . "Not my bag."
    Time stops: the felt pen recording, the magazine, the tape
recorders, my terrified mind stops remembering it, while Teresa
Juarez's voice loud butches me from a floor mike center of the
room, a bully for all the correct political reasons. Five hundred
people looking at me. Are you a lesbian? Everything pauses,
faces look up in terrible silence, I hear them not breathe. That

*word in public, the word I waited half a lifetime to hear. Finally
I am accused. "Say it. Say you are a lesbian." Yes I said. Yes.
Because I know what she means. The line goes inflexible as a
fascist edict, that bisexuality is a cop-out. Yes I said yes I am a
lesbian. It was the last strength I had.*

Kate Millett
Flying, Alfred A. Knopf, 1974

*I have been a selfish being all my life, in practice, though not
in principle.*

Jane Austen

*The trouble with me is that I am a vindictive old shanty-Irish
bitch.*

Eleanor (Cissy) Patterson
Publisher and sole owner,
Washington D.C. Times Herald,
Director, Chicago Tribune Company, N.Y.
Daily News Company and all affiliated Co.

Chapter Two

WHAT WOMEN SAY ABOUT BEING A WOMAN

When I was a little girl growing up in suburbia in the 1930's I secretly didn't think I was going to grow up to be a woman. I was not too clear about biology, but I knew something would happen to turn me into a man. Then I could dress up each morning and be driven to the railroad station to catch the commuter train into the City, have an exciting day, eat lunch out in a restaurant, and have everybody wait dinner for me until I came home to tell them about my day's adventures.

Being a man was where the action was — that was for me. Men's clothes had pockets which held lots of money, large gold watches, and sometimes candy. And men brought newspapers home with them; the newspapers I was learning to read from, eschewing the pallid lives of Dick and Jane.

With menstruation came the knowledge that I was turning out to be a woman after all. It took time to adjust to this. Getting into college helped. Four years of sitting in chapel and having the dean tell us, "You are the cream of the crop — the best in the country," had its effects; along with buying clothes that had many pockets.

I found I was good at business. A rising star has no gender, at least at the lower corporate levels. Marriage and three children saw me into the beginnings of the women's movement, with its wonderful message that the world was out there for everybody who wanted it. I did.

Here's what other women say . . .

From birth to age eighteen a girl needs good parents. From eighteen to thirty-five she needs good looks. From thirty-five to fifty-five she needs a good personality. From fifty-five on she needs good cash.

Sophie Tucker
Entertainer

There are two ways of spreading the light: to be the candle or the mirror that reflects it.

Edith Wharton, 1862 - 1937
Writer

We do not understand the psychology of women because women have not articulated their experience.

Anais Nin
Poet, writer

A perfectly normal person is rare in our civilization.

Dr. Karen Horney
Psychologist, founder of the
Karen Horney Institute

Janet Harris writes of growing up in the 1940's:

> *Boys liked girls who were "well groomed," according to the magazines. I worried about BO, gargled with Listerine, bought little tins of Mum with my allowance money. I shaved my legs secretly with my father's Remington. I wrote to Max Factor of Hollywood for a makeup kit containing a tiny packet of powder and a minute lipstick "coordinated" to my "individual coloring." (One of the women I interviewed for this book told me she even sent away for a sample of Absorbine, Jr., in case it was athlete's foot that was keeping her from being prom queen. "I would have drunk it," she told me.)*

Janet Harris
The Prime of Ms America,   G.P. Putnam

Sophie Tucker

Hedy Lamarr

Hedy Lamarr gained international notoriety for her nude scene
in the German film, "Ecstacy," and went on to become an
erotic symbol for American film-goers. She developed a breath-
less glamour, lips moist and slightly parted, eyes dewy and
unblinking, her whole being waiting for her man. And in later
years she said in an interview:

> *Any girl can be glamourous. All you have to do is stand
> still and look stupid.*

Another Hollywood actress from the same era spoke of
beauty . . .

> *Beauty does not come with creams and lotions. God can
> give us beauty, but whether that beauty remains or changes
> is determined by our thoughts and deeds. A woman who
> leads a lazy life will reflect it in her face.*
>
> Dolores Del Rio
People, August 16, 1976

Referring to appearance, Tallulah Bankhead concluded:

> *There's less in this than meets the eye . . .*

From Dorothy Parker:

> *Brevity is the soul of lingerie.*

*There is only one proper way to wear a beautiful dress:
to forget you are wearing it.*

Mme. Girardin

Vanity, like murder, will out.

Hannah Cowley, 1743 - 1809
American writer

You know you're getting fat when you step on a dog's tail

and he dies. Or when you get up from a metal chair and have to fluff it up . . .

Elayne Boosler
Comic, 1976

Edna Woolman Chase, Vogue's editor for thirty-eight years, cautioned women:

Fashion can be bought, style one must possess. I have seen a Texas cowboy swing himself into his saddle with more real elegance, more style than many gentlemen on the hunting field . . .

Edna Woolman Chase
Always In Vogue, Doubleday, 1954

Diana Vreeland, Special Consultant to the Costume Institute of the Metropolitan Museum — herself a past editor of Vogue, adds:

. . . the only real elegance is in the mind; if you've got that, the rest really comes from it.

Newsweek, December, 1962

A gossip is one who talks to you about others, a bore is one who talks to you about himself, and a brilliant conversationalist is one who talks to you about yourself.

Lisa Kirk
Singer, entertainer

One learns in life to keep silent and draw one's own conclusions.

Cornelia Otis Skinner
Writer

Contemporary etiquette authority Marjabelle Stewart advises:
Good manners take you where money can't go.

Marjabelle Stewart
White Gloves and Party Manners

*We women do talk too much, but even then we don't tell half
we know.*

Lady Nancy Astor
First woman to sit in
British Parliament, 1919 - 1945

Anne Morrow Lindberg, writer and wife of Charles Lindberg,
explored being a woman in her book *A Gift From The Sea.*
She wrote:
*I believe that what a woman resents is not so much giving
herself in pieces as giving herself purposelessly.*

I think housework is the reason most women go to the office.
Heloise
Heloise's Household Hints

English feminist Mary Wollstonecraft (Shelley), speaking
for education for women, in 1792:
*It is hardly surprising that women concentrate on the way
they look instead of what was in their minds since not
much has been put in their minds to begin with.*

*It occurred to me when I was thirteen and wearing white gloves
and Mary Janes and going to dancing school, that no one should
have to dance backwards all their lives.*

Jill Ruckelshaus
Discussing discrimination
1973

In 1912, three years after graduating from college, anthro-
pologist Ruth Benedict wrote despairingly of the future . . .
*So much of the trouble is because I am a woman. To me
it seems a very terrible thing to be a woman. There is one
crown which perhaps is worth it all — a great love, a quiet
home, and children. We all know that is all that is worth-*

while, and yet we must peg away, showing off our wares on the market if we have money, or manufacturing careers for ourselves if we haven't. We have not the motive to prepare ourselves for a "life-work" of teaching, of social work — we know that we would lay it down with hallelujah in the height of our success, to make a home for the right man.

And all the time in the background of our consciousness rings the warning that perhaps the right man will never come. A great love is given to very few. Perhaps this make-shift time filler of a job is our life work after all.

Two years later, 1914, she married Stanley Benedict; nine years later, at age thirty-four she enrolled at Columbia and began studying anthropology.

> Margaret Mead
> *Ruth Benedict,*
> Columbia University Press

(Sarah) Margaret Fuller, 1810 - 1850, was a forerunner of American feminists. Educated in the classics, she became an intellectual leader, and in 1844 accepted publisher Horace Greeley's invitation to become literary editor of the New York Tribune. In 1846 she went to Italy, had a son by an Italian Count whom she later married, and with him participated in the Italian Revolution of 1848 - 49. She was drowned in a shipwreck, while returning to America in 1850. Her book *Women in the Nineteenth Century* (1845) was hailed as the first mature consideration of Feminism by an American. She wrote:

In order that she may be able to give her hand with dignity, she (woman) must be able to stand alone.

In nine cases out of ten, a woman had better show more affection than she feels.

> Jane Austen

Charlotte Perkins Gilman was the best known American

radical feminist philosopher of the 1880's - 1890's. In her
book *Women and Economics*, published in 1898, she wrote:
> *There is no female mind. The brain is not an organ of*
> *sex. As well speak of a female liver.*

Marion Mitchell, who came to teach astronomy at Vassar
College in 1865, advised her students:
> *Study as if you were going to live forever; live as if you*
> *were going to die tomorrow.*

Contemporary writer Elizabeth Janeway writes:
> *If the old role tells women "You're inferior," it also offers*
> *a definition of limited but possible success. If your daughters*
> *are pretty, popular and married young, if your sons get good*
> *jobs, and if your husband comes home to dinner every night,*
> *you've reached your goal and you can relax. Isn't the*
> *(women's) movement questioning this definition of success?*
> *Yes. Isn't it putting down women who have striven for such*
> *success? No.*
>
> Elizabeth Janeway
> *Between Myth and Morning*

> *Listening to women call themselves "happy housewives" is*
> *oftentimes a little like watching birds whose wings have been*
> *clipped. Some women do like it, or adjust to it, but many go*
> *on making heartbreaking attempts to fly all their lives.*
>
> Dale Carlson
> *Girls Are Equal Too,* 1976

The First National Women's Rights Convention, held in pre-Civil
War 1851, was stunned when the six-foot black abolitionist
Sojourner Truth addressed the meeting:
> *Well, children, where there is so much racket there must be*
> *something out of kilter. I think that betwixt the niggers of*
> *the South and the women of the North, all talking about*
> *rights, the white men will be in a fix pretty soon. But what's*

all this here talking about?

That man over there say that a woman needs to be helped into carriages, and lifted over ditches, and to have the best place everywhere. Nobody ever helped me into carriages, or over mud puddles, or gives me a best place . . . and ain't I a woman? Look at me. Look at my arm: I have plowed and planted and gathered into barns, and no man could head me . . . and ain't I a woman? I could work as much and eat as much as a man when I could get it, and bear the lash as well . . . and ain't I a woman? I have borned thirteen children and seen most all sold off into slavery. And when I cried out with a mother's grief, none but Jesus heard . . . and ain't I a woman? Then they talks about this thing in the head; what this they call it?

("Intellect" somebody whispered.) That's it, honey, What's that got to do with women's rights or nigger's rights? If my cup won't hold but a pint, and yours holds a quart, wouldn't you be mean not to let me have my little half-measure full?

Then that little man in black, he says women can't have as much rights as men, because Christ wasn't a woman! Where did your Christ come from? Where did your Christ come from? From God and a woman! Man had nothing to do with him . . . if the first woman God ever made was strong enough to turn the world upside down all alone, these women together ought to be able to turn it back, and get it right side up again! And now they is asking to do it, the men better let them.

Obliged to you for hearing on me, and now ole Soujourner hasn't got nothing more to say.

Judith Papachristou
Women Together

In 1969, a New York City radical feminists group echoed many of these points in the Redstocking Manifesto:

VI. We identify with all women. We define our best interest as that of the poorest, most brutally exploited women.

We repudiate all economic, racial, educational or

status privileges that divide us from other women. We are determined to recognize and eliminate any prejudice we may hold against other women.

We are committed to achieving internal democracy. We will do whatever is necessary to ensure that every woman in our movement has an equal chance to participate, assume responsibility, and develop her political potential.

VII. We call on all our sisters to unite with us in struggle.

We call on all men to give up their male privileges and support women's liberation in the interests of our humanity and their own.

In fighting for our liberation we will always take the side of women against their oppressors. We will not ask what is "revolutionary" or "reformist" only what is good for women.

The time for individual skirmishes has passed. This time we are going all the way.

Chapter Three

WHAT WOMEN SAY ABOUT OTHER WOMEN

I can't think of a time in my life when women have not been my umbilical cord to reality, perhaps even survival.

I belonged to the team, and my sense of belonging cushioned disasters in other parts of my life. When triumphs were to be celebrated, I turned to my women friends to be joyful; there was no part of me I had to hide from them.

I hope my daughters can say this about all human beings.

Here's what women say about other women . . .

Frances Farmer, writing about her friend Jean Ratcliffe:
> . . . *and I have learned that to have a good friend is the purest of all God's gifts, for it is a love that has no exchange of payment. It is not inherited, as with a family. It is not compelling, as with a child. And it has no means of physical pleasure, as with a mate. It is, therefore, an indescribable bond that brings with it a far deeper devotion than all the others.*

> Frances Farmer
> *Will There Really Be a Morning,*
> G. P. Putnam

Women like other women fine. The more feminine she is, the more comfortable a woman feels with her own sex. It is only the occasional and therefore noticeable adventuress who refuses to make friends with us.

> Phyllis McGinley
> *The Province of the Heart*

Historian Linda De Pauw speaking about our foremothers:
> *You have to consider what it must have been like for Abigail Adams, five months pregnant, learning that her husband was going to Philadelphia (to attend the Continental Congress) where he was likely to commit a crime that would get him hanged. She was proud of him, but the fact that she broke down in tears is something we can all identify with.*

Writer Diane de Dubovay, quoting an "anonymous, stylish, forty-ish woman":
> *The men in my life may come and go, but I wouldn't jeopardize the few close friendships I have with women for anything — because I know that, no matter what happens, they'll always be there. It was my close women friends, in fact, who introduced me to both of my husbands.*

> Vogue, July, 1975

Frances Farmer

Jeanne Moreau

What I wanted to show in my films was, precisely how when
women are together . . . bitterness doesn't exist. There is a
lightness in their relations, even when their feelings are very
strong, even when they are speaking of serious things . . .
with men who are my friends I have had to pass beyond
the stage of sexuality, and we have had to pass through that
stage first.

> Jeanne Moreau
> French filmmaker and actress
> (Judith Thurman, MS, January, 1977)

Humorist Erma Bombeck offers her description of what
a friend is:

> *. . . a friend doesn't go on a diet when* you *are fat. A friend*
> *never defends a husband who gets his wife an electric*
> *skillet for her birthday. A friend will tell you she saw your*
> *old boy friend — and he's a priest. A friend will lie about*
> *your home permanent and threaten to kill anyone who*
> *tries to come into a room where you are trying on bathing*
> *suits. But, most of all, a friend will not make every minute*
> *of every day count and foul it up for the rest of us.*

> Erma Bombeck
> *The Grass Is Always Greener Over the Septic Tank*

Women pilots were surefire newspaper copy in the 1930's, and
a lot of words were put into building up a supposed feud between
Amelia Earhart and Ruth Nichols.

> *Many newspaper articles . . . discussed the supposed rivalry*
> *between Amelia and me. I have no hesitation in stating*
> *that they were exaggerated or slanted or untrue. Both of*
> *us were intent on flying careers. Both of us were out after*
> *every record we could get . . . We remained good friends*
> *throughout all our competitions . . . We were united by a*
> *common bond of interest. We spoke each other's*
> *language — and that was the language of pioneer women*
> *of the air.*

> Ruth Nichols
> *Wings For Life*

I also find most women are being more encouraging to other women. People used to say to me, "Do you find that women are not your supporters?" Women are my greatest supporters. *The only ones who are not are women who are somehow threatened by another who is successful at her work. In part, it has been because of the Women's Movement — the idea that if you stayed at home there must be something wrong with you. That's the only destructive part of the Women's Movement, and it was not something they did deliberately. And it will change. Women will find confidence in themselves, in the home as well, if they want that.*

The young woman knows where she's at. There's no problem there. My generation is somewhat torn — not just the women, but the men. We know what we should feel intellectually; and yet, emotionally we've been brought up totally different. And it's very hard to live by both. Especially for men and women who find themselves, in their 30's or 40's or even 50's, newly single and don't know which approach they should take.

It's a wonderful time to be a woman if you have courage and something of your own; otherwise it can be frightening. Either something you can do of your own, or some money of your own, or some husband of your own, or something that gives you a feeling of security. Otherwise it's a turbulent time. But it is a time when a woman can have anything and everything if she has the courage and this other.

A woman can be anything. She can be traditionally feminine and that's all right; she can work, she can stay at home; she can be aggressive, she can be passive; she can be any way she wants with a man. But whenever there are the kinds of choices that there are today, unless you have some solid base, life can be frightening.

Barbara Walters
Vogue, June, 1975

English feminist Ida Alexa Ross Wylie, reminiscing about her experiences in the English Suffragette Movement, prior to World War I:

For two years of wild and sometimes dangerous adventure, I worked and fought alongside vigorous, happy, well-ad-

*justed women who laughed instead of tittering, who walked
instead of teetering, who could out-fast Gandhi and come
out with a grin and a jest. I slept on hard floors between
elderly duchesses, stout cooks, and shopgirls . . . We were
often tired, hurt and frightened. But we were content as we
had never been. We shared a joy of life that we had never
known. Most of my fellow fighters were wives and mothers.
And strong things happened to their domestic life. Husbands
came home at night with a new eagerness . . . As for children,
their attitude changed rapidly from one of affectionate
toleration for poor, darling mother to one of wide wonder.
Released from the smother of mother love, for she was too
busy to be more than casually concerned with them, they
discovered that they liked her. She was a great sport. She
had guts . . .*

Harper's, November, 1945

Norah Ephron interviews Linda Lovelace, star of porno movie
"Deep Throat":

Ephron: Why do you shave off your pubic hair in the film?

Lovelace: I always do it. I like it.

Ephron: But why do you like it?

Lovelace: Well, it's kinda hot in Texas.

Ephron: Well, I think it's weird.

Lovelace: Weird? Why?

Ephron: Well, I don't know anyone who does that.

Lovelace: Now you do.

Norah Ephron
Crazy Salad

*. . . The twelve year old daughter of emancipated parents, who
asked her Ma, "What's a prostitute?" Ma explained conscientiously,
finishing off with, "She's the kind of woman who does it for
money." "Oh," said her darling daughter, "you mean she's a
whore. . ."*

Vogue, March, 1975

I think if women would indulge more freely in vituperation, they would enjoy ten times the health they do. It seems to me they are suffering from repression.
> Elizabeth Cady Stanton
> American feminist
> 1859

When a pushy tourist rang Georgia O'Keefe's doorbell and demanded to see the artist, O'Keefe stepped out, snapped, "All right. Frontside," — and, turning, "Backside," and then, "Goodbye."

I have discovered that our great favorite, Miss Austen, is my countryman . . . with whom Mama, before her marriage, was acquainted. Mama says that she was then the prettiest, silliest, most affected, husband-hunting butterfly she ever remembers.
> Mary Russell Mitford
> Letter to a friend, April 3, 1815

Margaret Halsey describing a woman:
> *. . . she blushed like a well-trained sunrise.*
> > Margaret Halsey
> > *With Malice Toward Some*

Ethel Merman, on Mary Martin:
> *She's O.K. if you like talent . . .*

Republican Congresswoman Jeanette Rankin, to birth control pioneer Margaret Sanger, at a post-World War II international conference on birth control:
> *All you talk about is vaginas, vaginas, vaginas. I'm getting out of here.*

*If all the girls at a Yale weekend were laid end to end I wouldn't
be a bit surprised.*
> Dorothy Parker

Actress Simone Signoret commenting on rumors linking her
husband, Yves Montand, with Marilyn Monroe:
> *If Marilyn is in love with my husband it proves she has
> good taste, for I am in love with him, too.*
>> New York Journal American,
>> November 14, 1960

French writer Colette advised her daughter:
> *You will do foolish things, but do them with enthusiasm.*

*Never grow a wishbone, daughter, where your backbone
ought to be.*
> Clementine Paddleford,
> Food authority
> Quoting advice from her mother, 1958

Writer Anita Loos speaks about her mother:
> *Like most extremely innocent people, she was obsessed
> by sex — not as a diversion (God forbid). She saw all
> females as constant objects of attack, while at the same
> time she never trusted me and wasn't at all sure I wouldn't
> be ready to cooperate in that sort of shady deal.*
>> Anita Loos
>> *Kiss Hollywood Goodbye*

Goethe's mother, Katherine Elizabeth Goethe, suggested:
> *. . . always look cheerful, that makes people feel good
> and doesn't cost anything.*

Then there are the great old phrases Everybody's Mother repeated and repeated and repeated . . .

Stand up straight . . . hold your stomach in.

Always put paper on the seat.

Put some lipstick on! Comb your hair! You never know who you might meet.

. . . if you smile you'd be as beautiful as anybody.

Remember who you are. You're too good for them.

It's just as easy to fall in love with a rich man as it is a poor man.

That's nice dear, but is he Jewish?
       Catholic?
       Chinese?
       Black?
       Italian?
       Employed?

Remember, man is the hunter.

Keep your knees together and keep your skirt well pulled down.

You wait for a man, you wait your whole life.

Chapter Four

WHAT WOMEN SAY ABOUT WORKING

When I think about work or career, three occurrences come
to mind that have been major influences on my attitudes and
my actions . . .

The first "real" job I ever had was in 1951. I worked in a
summer theatre in Fall River, Massachusetts, and was paid
seventy-five dollars a week. Each Friday when I opened my
brown pay envelope I would be filled with wonder at the tens
and five within. Didn't they know I would have gladly worked
for nothing? To be able to hang around a theatre was reward
enough.

The second occurrence dates back to college. The gentleman
in my life was a serious soul, dedicated to his chosen profession.
I, on the other hand, liked almost everything that came by. He
was annoyed by this, and regularly denounced me for being a
hopeless dilletante. I believed him, and skulked through the 50's
and into the 60's feeling guilty about being into a little bit of
everything. Then John Lindsay became mayor of New York City,
bringing with him the concept of the "renaissance person."
Suddenly it was alright to have a broad spectrum of accom-
plishments. I was O.K. — nay, I was *IN.*

The last "happening" was in Chicago during a home furnish-
ings market week, in the mid-50's. I was part of a group doing
market coverage for a New York company — a corporation
to which Dorothy Liebes, the legendary colorist and handweaver,
was a consultant. She became ill at the market, and was ordered
to bed. I, as the junior member of our team, was ordered to go
sit with Dorothy in case she needed anything. For several days
she talked and I listened, and came away with her business advice:
"Never work for only one company at a time. Have many small
incomes coming from many different companies — *then* you can
call your soul your own."

*How many cares one loses when one decides not to be
something, but to be someone.*

> Coco Chanel
> Fashion designer
> 1955

*You must learn day by day, year by year, to broaden your
horizon. The more things you love, the more you are
interested in, the more you enjoy, the more you are indignant
about — the more you have left when anything happens.*

> Ethel Barrymore

*In many ways we have it easier. If a woman picks up a pencil
everybody says, "Isn't that fantastic!"*

> Maureen Lambray
> Fashion photographer
> Mademoiselle, December, 1976

Returning from a year of retirement, ballerina Cynthia Gregory
said:

> *I am back because ballet is what I do best. I had begun
> to hate dancing. For the first time, dancing was like an
> execution. I couldn't remember the roles I was learning.
> At some time every dancer wonders if she can go on.
> I couldn't.*

> People, January 10, 1977

Sarah Caldwell began her career as a conductor in Boston, where
she founded the Boston Opera Company. She has conducted
at the Metropolitan Opera Company, N.Y.C., and is noted for
staging avant garde opera. She speaks of her work:

> *Once in a while, when everything is just right, there is
> a moment of magic. People can live on moments of magic.*

Sarah Caldwell

If I read a book and it makes my whole body so cold no fire can ever warm me, I know that it is poetry. If I feel physically as if the top of my head were taken off, I know it is poetry. These are the only ways I know it. Is there any other way?

Emily Dickinson

One hopes every picture will be a new birth, a fresh experience within a growing framework.

Helen Frankenthaler
Contemporary American artist

Because of the nature of my career, the constant striving, I never feel that I've arrived. There's always so much more to do. I'm constantly amazed at how much the body can do — much more than anyone thinks. Each step opens whole new doors. Other dancers have asked me if I get bored. I don't, I don't get bored at all. There's always another possibility.

Eleanor D'Antuono
Dancer, American Ballet Theatre

Brigadier General Jeanne M. Holm, U.S. Army Air Force, speaks about her career:

I've never felt that I was held back because I was a woman. That doesn't mean that everybody has had this experience — in some ways I simply lucked out.

. . . my funniest experiences seem to come from reaction to the uniform. Some stare because they see few women generals. Others think that perhaps I'm an airline stewardess. Once, on a commercial airliner, a little old lady mistook me for the pilot. She jumped up and said, "If she's flying this thing, I'm getting off . . ."

Suzanne Seed
Saturday's Children,
Bantam

Whatever women do they must do twice as well as men to
be thought half as good. Luckily, this is not difficult.

Charlotte Whitton
Mayor of Ottawa, Canada,
June, 1963

Men see work as a series of tasks to be completed, all adding up
to something; women often look at a job as an endless stream of
work, with no beginning, middle or end.

Drs. Margaret Henning and Anne Jardin
The Managerial Woman

Radcliffe College President Matina Horner speaking of fear
of success:

We found that at the point women were closing the gap
between the amount of money they made, relative to
the significant male in their lives, many of them got
pregnant as a coping strategy.

People, June 21, 1976

How we are fallen! Fallen by mistaken rules
And Education's more than Nature's fools;
Debarred from all improvement of the mind
And to be dull, expected and designed
And if someone would soar above the rest,
With warmer fancy and ambitions pressed,
So strong the opposing faction still appears,
the hopes to thrive can ne'er outweigh the fears.

Lady Winchilsea
Seventeenth Century Englishwoman

Feminist lawyer Florynce Kennedy — on employment:

There are very few jobs that actually require a penis
or vagina. All other jobs should be open to everybody.

Lisa Taylor

Museum Director Lisa Taylor, speaking about the Metamorphosis
show that reopened the Cooper-Hewitt Museum:

Nobody knows who made the first piece of cloth and where
— it's as important to design as the wheel, and maybe more.
So we do a lot of things to that piece of cloth. If you put it
on a pole it becomes a flag, if you decorate the flag it repre-
sents a specific nation, or can be a yacht's ensign. And
there the flag is carried through to the semaphore and it be-
comes a language, and then you put it on two poles and it
becomes a sail. Or, a piece of cloth becomes a toga or
an Indian sari or Western, architecturally-constructed clothes.
In the West, time is spent making clothes, in other cultures
the time is spent in elaborate procedures putting them on.
And then there is a piece of cloth that is a house, or the
whole question of portability, from a mailbag to a furoshiki.
And what about the cloth used to blow your nose or wipe
your car?

When asked how she could be both a member of Congress and
a mother, Pat Schroeder says:

I have a brain and a uterus and I use both.

Replying to criticism of her appointment by Franklin Delano
Roosevelt to be U.S. Secretary of Labor (1933), Frances Perkins
said:

Being a woman has only bothered me in climbing trees.

Henry Kissinger to Raquel Welch:

HK: Raquel, I've got a problem. What does an ex-
Secretary of State do?

RW: Henry, I've got the same problem. What does an
ex-sex symbol do?

People, June 21, 1976

Lawyer Florynce Kennedy speaking about employment and
homemakers:

You get a hundred dollars a week for filing, and a
hundred dollars a night for fucking, but you don't get
nuthin' for filing, and fucking, and cleaning, and
cooking, and washing, and ironing, and chauffering, and
nursing, and sewing, and . . .

Florynce Kennedy
Color Me Flo,
Prentice-Hall

. . . the fault, dear brothers, lies not in our stars, our hormones,
our menstrual or our empty internal spaces, but in our institutions
and our education — education understood to include everything
that happens to us from the moment we enter this world of
meaningful symbols, signs, and signals. The miracle is, in fact,
that given the overwhelming odds against women, or blacks, that
so many of both have managed to achieve so much sheer
excellence, in those bailiwicks of white masculine prerogatives
like science, politics or the arts.

Linda Nochlin
Why Have There Been
No Great Women Artists

I like earning money. I like it when companies seek me out
and sign me up to design no matter what — sheets, yard goods,
glassware, scarves, wallpaper, table linen, valentines. I like being
every year in greater demand. I like having to face week after
week my all but impossible deadlines. The fame you earn has
a different taste from the fame that is forced upon you.

Gloria Vanderbilt
Vogue, June, 1975

I got all the schooling any actress needs. That is, I learned to
write enough to sign contracts.

Hermione Gingold

Gloria Vanderbilt

When you are talking to men in business, they all think you're tough and mean if you disagree with them, and they wouldn't think that if it were another man. An art director said to me, "You have no heart!" I wouldn't do what he wanted and he said "You have no heart!" I couldn't help it but I broke out laughing, and he hung up on me. It wasn't a love affair. It was business. It had nothing to do with my heart one way or the other.

Eileen Ford
Author and co-owner,
Ford Model Agency
People, January 16, 1977

Who me, work, in an office? I can't even type.

Elizabeth Ray
Washington, D.C.

I like the sport, and know I've got the ability. That's where the money is.

Anne Meyers
UCLA championship
basketball player

When I found out an engineer went into the big wide world and made money while the physicist stayed in the lab, I opted for the money.

Senior nuclear reactor
operator Roberta Kankus,
People, July 26, 1976

Roz Kelly, the actress who played Pinky Tuscadero in "Happy Days," speaks of her early career struggles:

> *... singing, and dancing my way through a rotten childhood ... I have a list of restaurant and coffee shop credits as long as that of my unreleased movies ... (and the released movies) probably shown in those places where you drop a quarter in the slot.*

Sure, I'm hot as a pistol now. But every offer is the same. All they want is tits and ass, tits and ass. If I hold out for something meaningful, I might never work again.

> Valerie Perrine
> Actress

Who said you should be happy? Do your work.

> Colette

Idle hands are the Devil's workshop.

> Everybody's Mother

When asked what she had on when doing her calendar modelling, Marilyn Monroe replied:
  "the radio."

For an actress to be a success she must have the face of Venus, the brains of Minerva, the grace of Terpsichore, the memory of Macauley, the figure of Juno, and the hide of a rhinoceros.

> Ethel Barrymore

A bright smile has compensated for many a vocal flaw in a concert.

> Gladys Swarthout

Gypsy Rose Lee, speaking of her TV debut:
  All they wanted of me were head shots. That certainly seemed strange. Nobody's ever paid attention to my face before.

Most men are afraid of opera singers. They think of them as people in another world. So I say I'm in the lingerie line. That puts them at their ease.

> Blanche Thebom
> Opera singer

Twyla Tharp

Dancing is like bank robbery. It takes split-second timing.
> Twyla Tharp
> Choreographer and dancer
> MS, December, 1976

Oceanographer Judy Joye, discussing the hazards of her career:
> *Some underwater animals are attracted by bright colors*
> *such as white, orange or yellow. One of my funniest*
> *experiences involved a large, 100 pound turtle that was*
> *attracted to the bright wires attached to my underwater*
> *camera. He grabbed them in his mouth and began chewing.*
> *Well, I knew better than to try taking food from an animal's*
> *mouth, but this camera had cost nearly a thousand dollars!*
> *I couldn't let him eat it so I began pulling the wires from*
> *him. He got very angry and grabbed my foot in his mouth.*
> *It was quite a scuffle, and I had to put both hands around*
> *his throat and begin choking him before he would let go.*

> Suzanne Seed
> *Saturday's Child,* Bantam

So I was sitting here, right here, looking at television one night
(in 1966). And Jack Paar was telling a dirty joke. And they
broke in, right in the middle, and this ad said, "Join the Peace
Corps. Age is no problem." And I said, "Well." Never thinking
I would go. I wrote that night for an application. I didn't tell
a soul. And I went downtown the next day, and Jimmy and
Billy were in the office. And I said, "Do y'all love me?" They
always know if I say that I want them to stop everything and
come mow the lawn. And Jimmy says, "Yeah." And Billy says,
"What in the hell do you want to do now, Momma?" That's the
difference in the two. And I said, "I'm going to join the Peace
Corps."

> Lillian Carter
> MS, October, 1976

My husband told me that if I wanted to write, and didn't, he'd
disown me, and from the minute we could afford household help,

we've had it by our joint decision. Most women don't have that luck and I know that.

Elizabeth Janeway

The only real physical effect that writing a novel has on the household is that I get so uninterested in cooking. My family can always tell when I'm well into a novel because the meals get very crummy.

Anne Tyler
Novelist

Singer and Composer Joni Mitchell talks about her work:
> *My family consists of pieces of work that go out into the world. Instead of hanging around for nineteen years they leave the nest early.*

The art of writing is the art of applying the seat of the pants to the seat of the chair.

Mary Heaton Vorse

The best time for planning a book is when you're doing the dishes.

Agatha Christie
Mystery writer

A young Katharine Hepburn, confronting her father about becoming an actress:
> *K.H.: I'm going to be an actress, Daddy.*
>
> *Father: You just want to show off — and get paid for it!*
>
> *K.H.: But Daddy, you let Mother make speeches for the suffragettes!*
>
> *Father: That was for a political purpose. This is just stupid vanity!*

K.H.: (tears)

*Father: All right! Here's fifty dollars. If you don't make
it to first base, that's the end!*

Charles Higham
Kate, Norton

Dorothy Parker, on working with Robert Benchley on
Vanity Fair:
> *He and I had an office so tiny that an inch smaller and
> it would have been adultery.*

*When I was six I made my mother a little hat — out of her
new blouse.*

Lilly Dache
December 3, 1954
Interview

Judith Viorst tells of writing her first poem at age eight:
> *An ode to my dead mother and father, who were both
> alive and pretty pissed off.*

Juanita Kreps, U.S. Secretary of Commerce, speaks of her career:
> *First of all, it was not luck. Even after I had a Ph.D. from
> Duke and had been teaching other places, I went back and
> took a part-time job. I had a degree from that place and
> had four or five years of teaching and was then thirty-five
> years old. And Duke started me as a visiting part-time
> instructor. And then I had to go on to visiting part-time
> assistant professor, and the inching up to full professor
> was very, very slow.*
>   *... But I must say in retrospect, I couldn't do it
> again. And I would take the place apart if I saw that sort
> of thing happening to my own daughter.*

I did this reading at the Library of Congress once. It was a great honor. Next day I was ironing, and I said, "What is this great poet doing ironing?" The kids laughed, and said, "Are you crazy?" and I came back to earth.

Lucille Clifton
Poet
MS, October, 1976

Eager TV interviewer to actress and model Lauren Hutton:
> *Why Lauren Hutton on twenty-two Vogue covers?*
> *Why Lauren Hutton with a big contract with Revlon?*
> *Why you and not any one of the other beautiful girls?*
> *Was it somebody you knew? Was it luck? Chutzpah?*

> *Lauren Hutton: (sarcastically) I fucked around.*

Dorothy Parker to publisher Harold Ross, on missing a New Yorker deadline:
> *Somebody was using the pencil.*

If I am controversial, it is because I fight for what I think is right, because I am honest, and when it comes to art, I say what I think. Perhaps that is my greatest fault — perhaps I should hypocritically conceal my thoughts, should play diplomat and butter up whatever management I am under.

No, I cannot do this. I am a fighter, for my art. I will fight to the teeth anyone who says I am not an honest laborer for the art of music. I am a noncomformist — but look at the lives of all great artists, singers. Have they been conformist? Did Caruso conform, even at the cost of his reputation? Was Melba a conformist? No!

I am perhaps what you would call a "lone wolf." They say Maria Callas is like the horse: you can lead it to water, but you can't make it drink. And Callas does not drink dirty water.

Maria Callas
1963

I never practice, I always play.

> Wanda Landowska
> Harpsichordist

I have never wanted to be anything but a gymnast. Maybe it is dangerous — but when you start thinking of danger, you might as well give up.

> Olga Korbut
> People, July 19, 1976

They're fancy talkers about themselves, writers. If I had to give young writers advice, I would say don't listen to writers talking about writing or themselves.

> Lillian Hellman

To me the sea is like a person — like a child that I've known a long time. It sounds crazy, I know, but when I swim in the sea I talk to it. I never feel alone when I'm out there.

> Gertrude Ederle
> First woman to swim
> the English Channel

Lilli Palmer, reminiscing about working with her drama coach, the legendary Elsa Schreiber:

> *"Don't show me your talent" became the leitmotif of my next 2 years. I loved showing my talent; I couldn't wait to demonstrate how clever I was, how well worth my salary. I had to learn that a good actor, like an iceberg, reveals only a small part of his ability on the surface. You suggest; you don't serve on a platter. You hold back. You don't expose it all to view. That's the way to put the audience's imagination to work.*

> Lilli Palmer
> *Change Lobsters and Dance,*
> Macmillan

*I learned how to conquer all fear of riding when I was still
in my teens. The scariest experience I've had was when I was
eighteen; I had a mild form of breast cancer, which the doctors
were able to cure without surgery. I feel I don't have much
else to fear after that. For luck I wear an orange bra, and that
keeps me from worrying about things.*

> Debbie Lawler
> Professional motorcycle jumper
> *The Flying Angel*

Nina Simone speaks ruefully about changing careers:
> *It's time to take a look at my failures and stop calling them
> successes. Now I can start working at something that can
> use me best.*

*Dancing is such a despised and dishonored trade that if you tell
a doctor or a lawyer you do choreography he'll look at you as if
you were a hummingbird. Dancers don't get invited to visit people.
It is assumed a boy dancer will run off with the spoons and a girl
with the head of the house.*

> Agnes De Mille
> Life, November 15, 1963

*Everywhere I go I'm asked if I think the universities stifle writers.
My opinion is that they don't stifle enough of them. There's
many a best-seller that could have been prevented by a good
teacher.*

> Flannery O'Connor
> *The Nature and Aim of Fiction*

*I feel depressed, invaded by the past because my writing forces
me to remember, because that is the source of my stories. If only
I could create fiction out of the present, but the present is sacred
to me, to be lived, to be passionately absorbed but not transfig-*

ured into fiction, to be preserved faithfully in my diary.
The alchemy of fiction is, for me, an act of embalming.

Anais Nin
Diary of Anais Nin, Volume V,
Harcourt Brace Jovanovich

Eileen Shanahan of the New York Times comments on her field:
A reporter who is liked is a reporter who has been had.

Any woman who tells you having your own career or own
identity is enough, she no longer needs a man, either knows
something I don't know or has taken up with women.

Barbara Howar
People, May 3, 1976

The only thing I like about being an actress is acting.

Elizabeth Ashley

Lily Tomlin, speaking about going to the Oscar Awards Ceremony
(nominated for her performance in "Nashville"):
. . . then I got it in my mind to go in clown face and fright
wig in an evening dress, and if I won, I was going to say,
"I know I've been thought of as a comedienne all my life
and to be accepted as a dramatic actress is so . . ."

Sandy Dennis talking about her early acting style:
I think (my) mannerisms offended a tremendous number
of people. They were due to the fact that I didn't know
what I was doing.

People, August 11, 1976

Of one of my earlier books, someone said I wrote like a

disgruntled schoolteacher. I felt that was unjust. I wasn't
a schoolteacher.

Catherine Drinker Bowen
Family Portrait,
Atlantic, Little, Brown

In 1863, at age 48, Julia Cameron received the gift of a camera.
It was from her children, who hoped it would amuse her on
holiday. Her photographs more than document Victorian
England. They are described by New York Times Art Editor,
Hilton Kramer, as ". . . art of the most exquisite candor and
dignity."

In her memoir, *Annals of My Glass House,* she wrote:
. . . from the first moment I handled my lens with a tender
ardor, and it has become to be as a living thing, with voice
and memory and creative vigor . . . I longed to arrest all
beauty that came before me, and at length the longing has
been satisfied.

Never learn to do anything. If you don't learn you'll always
find someone else to do it.

Jane Clemens
Mother of Mark Twain

Writer Mary Roberts Rinehart, on rereading one of her earliest
mysteries, at eighty-one:
I'm having a wonderful time. I can't figure out who did
the killing.

When somebody says they're writing something with you in
mind, that's the end. I want them to write with Katherine
Cornell or Helen Hayes in mind and then let me have a go
at it.

Bea Lillie

I just made love to ten thousand people but now I'm going
home alone.

Janis Joplin

Bea Lillie

Chapter Five

WHAT WOMEN SAY ABOUT MOTHERHOOD

Do little girls still grow up wanting to be mommies? When I was little, and even not so little, there didn't seem to be anything else a little girl could grow up to be. But the joys of motherhood, as portrayed then, never bore out the realities I saw in all the houses on our block. This was joyful?

I found I was not alone, pondering the credibility gap. A lot of us arrived at the door of Lying-In Hospital, still trying to put the pieces together, while we were timing contractions. A year later we were able to conclude only that having a baby certainly did change one's life. Things got better or worse as the focus changed from "I" to "we" to "all of us." Babies grew into kids, teenagers, and young adults just as puppies and kittens turned into full grown cats and dogs. Life was enriched.

Should women have total choice about having babies? The advocates and opposers are equally positive of their stance. Margaret Sanger and others spent time in prisons for preaching birth control. I know very few women who have not had an abortion. And I know a few who should have had them; whose lives would have been bettered and lengthened. The right to choose seems so logical; then everyone can have whatever she wants.

I'm glad I had the babies I had, and glad I didn't have the ones I didn't want. I found I could do a lot of other things, too.

Here's how motherhood has seemed to other women.

The only thing that seems eternal and natural in motherhood is ambivalence.

Jane Lazarre
The Mother Knot

I have been asked if I had the choice again, would I have a child? This is an absurd question. I am not the same person I was before I had a child. That young woman would not understand me.

Susan Griffin
Momma: the newspaper for single mothers

To be a mother is not a trade. It's not even a duty. It's only one right among many.

Oriana Fallaci
Italian journalist, feminist
Letter to An Unborn Child

There is this to be said about little children: They keep you feeling old.

Jean Kerr
Writer and playwright
Penny Candy

Being a housewife and a mother is the biggest job in the world, but if it doesn't interest you, don't do it. It didn't interest me so I didn't do it. Anyway, I would have made a terrible parent. The first time my child didn't do what I wanted, I'd kill him.

Katharine Hepburn
People, October 11, 1976

Being a mother is a noble status, right? Right. So why does it change when you put "unwed" or "welfare" in front of it?

Florynce Kennedy
Lawyer, feminist

Jane Lazarre

In 1915, the first U.S. birth control organization, the National Birth Control League, was formed in New York by a group of women inspired by the arrest of Margaret Sanger and her husband, William, for violation of the laws against birth control literature. By 1917, about twenty such leagues were functioning in different parts of the country; ten years later thirty-seven thousand women belonged to the American Birth Control League. In 1920, Margaret Sanger wrote:

> *No woman can call herself free who does not own and control her body. No woman can call herself free until she can choose consciously whether she will or will not be a mother.*

Margaret Sanger
Woman and the New Race

India, 1967 — Peace Corp Worker Lillian Carter writes home to her family:

> *I've felt very deeply against family planning as I first saw it here, but now, I see little babies as small as mice, no food, no clothes, no nothing. They say nobody can make them practice family planning; it's God's work. Well! That's a damn lie! I'm sure my God doesn't want babies hatched like fish!*

A fire has been lighted which effects the basics, beginning with the family. It all started with the pill, of course. Not because it enabled women to avoid having children. That's the secondary aspect, no matter how convenient it may be. It was because, for the first time in the history of humanity, that decision belonged to women. And not only is the decision theirs, but in a sense they cannot avoid it, for not to make it is another way of making it.

Francoise Giroud
First French Secretary of State
for the Condition of Women
I Give You My Word,
Houghton Mifflin

Florynce Kennedy

If men could get pregnant, abortion would be a sacrament.
Florynce Kennedy
American feminist, lawyer

It sometimes happens, even in the best of families, that a baby is born. This is not necessarily cause for alarm. The important thing is to keep your wits about you and borrow some money.
Elinor Goulding Smith
The Complete Book of Absolutely Perfect Baby and Child Care

As an incentive to industry, enterprise and thrift, there isn't anything that can beat twins.

Florence Heald
Writer

Jean Kerr describes herself pregnant with twins:
I was square and looked like a refrigerator approaching.
Vogue, May, 1958

A number of years later Jean Kerr wrote:
. . . I am the mother of five sons and therefore have to go out a lot . . .

Gisella Heinemann

Writer Gisella Heinemann talks about giving birth to her daughter, Johanna:
As Dr. Given laid the baby across my stomach he said, "It's a girl," and I said, "Now I have a friend."

A baby is an alimentary canal with a loud voice at one end and no responsibility at the other.

Elizabeth I. Adamson

*Ronnie is calling. He is wet and I change him. It is rare there
is such a cry now. That time of motherhood is almost behind
me when the ear is not one's own but must always be racked
and listening for the child cry, the child call. We sit for a while
and I hold him, looking out over the city spread in charcoal
with its soft aisles of light. "Shoogily," he breathes and curls
closer. I carry him back to bed, asleep. Shoogily. A funny
word, a family word, inherited from Emily, invented by her
to say: comfort.*

> Tillie Olsen
> *Tell Me A Riddle*

*Personal success and parenting do not go well together. Your
career is your favorite child.*

> Jill Robinson
> Vogue, June, 1975

Writer Letty Cottin Pogrebin tells this anecdote:
> *One evening at the dinner table I question my children
> about their thoughts on motherhood.*
>
> *"Is that like Robin Hood?" asks my five-year-old son.*
>
> *One eight-year-old daughter assumes an angelic expres-
> sion and recites, "Motherhood is a great thing because a
> mother is a person's very best relative."*
>
> *"A mother is someone who looks good in hoods,"
> offers her twin sister, overjoyed at her own wit.*
>
> *My husband shifts the conversation to a more pressing
> problem; "Now let's see if we can't all agree," he begins
> patiently, "that a family in midtown Manhattan has no
> business buying a hunting dog."*

> MS, May, 1973

Hide your learning, daughter, as if it were a physical defect.
> Lady Mary Wortley Montagu, 1689 - 1762
> English poet

Indira Gandhi

*My sons . . . I was crazy about my sons and I think I've done a
super job in bringing them up. Today in fact they're two fine
and serious men. No, I've never understood women who, because
of their children, pose as victims and don't allow themselves any
other activities. It's not at all hard to reconcile the two things
if you organize your time intelligently. Even when my sons were
little I was working. I was a welfare worker for the Indian
Council for Child Welfare. I'll tell you a story. Rajiv was only
four years old at that time, and was going to kindergarten. One
day the mother of one of his little friends came to see us and
said in a sugary voice, "Oh, it must be sad for you to have no
time to spend with your little boy!" Rajiv roared like a lion:
"My mother spends more time with me than you spend with
your little boy, see! Your little boy says you always leave him
alone so you can play bridge!" I detest women who do nothing
and then play bridge.*

Indira Gandhi
Indian political leader
(Oriana Fallaci
Interviews)

*If we could learn how to utilize all the intelligence and patent
good will children are born with, instead of ignoring it — why —
there might be enough to go around!*

Dorothy Canfield Fisher
American writer

*Build better schoolrooms for "the boy"
Than cells and gibbets for "the man."*

Eliza Cook, 1818 - 1889
English poet

Mary Wollstonecraft Shelley, author of Frankenstein, asked
advice from a friend about schools to send her child to:

Discipline must come through liberty. Here is a great principle which is difficult for followers of the common school methods to understand. How shall one obtain discipline in a class of free children? Certainly in our system we have a concept of discipline very different from that commonly accepted. If discipline is founded upon liberty, the discipline itself must necessarily be active. *We do not consider an individual disciplined only when he has been rendered as artificially silent as a mute and as immovable as a paralytic. He is an individual* annihilated, *not* disciplined.

> Maria Montessori, 1870 -1952
> Italian educator

Writer Dale Carlson tells this story about her five-year-old daughter:

> . . . *the household had had quite a dose of women's liberation. But since my daughter is young, I had no real notion about how much of it was affecting her. That truly, in the deepest part of her, she understood, I saw during a game of charades.*
>
> *She pointed upward for the first part of the word in a movie title, and as our guess was incorrect, she began on the second part of the word. She made a rocking motion with her arms, as if to rock a baby. My son and I guessed words like mother, nurse, grandmother, nanny, while my daughter grew more and more impatient and puzzled. She didn't change her motion, but went on rocking harder than ever. Several times in a row she went over the title, first pointing upward, then making the rocking-the-baby motion. Finally we gave up, and she said, "Oh for goodness sake, it was so easy. 'The Godfather' is the answer. You were so*

Maria Montessori

busy thinking of mothers every time I rocked the baby,
that's why you didn't get it. Why couldn't you think of
fathers rocking a baby?"

Dale Carlson
Girls Are Equal Too

You see much more of your children once they leave home.

Lucille Ball

Eighty-two-year-old writer Florida Scott Maxwell is quoted:
No matter how old a mother is she watches her middle-
aged children for signs of improvement.

Gail Sheehy
Passages

Lucille Ball

Chapter Six

WHAT WOMEN SAY ABOUT MONEY

As for me, my periods of poverty were totally voluntary. Like many middle-classies, life among "the people" had an allure for me that could never be matched by a charge account at Bonwit Teller. As soon as I got out of college (high class, Ivy League) I hurried into the lower depths at top speed.

There I remained until my growing uneasiness surfaced and forced me to admit that I was there with false credentials. I had no stories to swap about how we made window curtains out of newspaper strips. I could not say that once a month we had dessert, apples dipped in honey. We never skipped out on a landlord because we owned the building.

Abandoning the underprivileged, I changed my tune and started to amass capital as fast as I could. It was nice to know I could do it. Years passed and I began to resent the amount of time it took to make money. My life was being spent doing dumb things to get money that I didn't even have time to enjoy. I withdrew from the corporate world, decided to work when I needed to, and settled back to wait for disaster to strike.

It didn't. But somehow the equation of money and time never worked out. If I had one, I didn't have the other. Then one day I found I was the beneficiary of an insurance policy which I hastened to collect.

With it came the ultimate truth: insurance money is the best kind of money a person can have.

Here's what other women have said about money . . .

It is extremely silly to submit to ill fortune.

> Lady Mary Wortley Montagu,
> 1689 - 1762
> Poet and wit; friend of
> Pope and Swift.

Well! Some people talk of morality, and some of religion, but give me a little snug property.

> Maria Edgeworth, 1767 - 1849
> British writer
> *The Absentee,* 1812

I do everything for a reason — most of the time the reason is money.

> Suzy Parker, 1955
> Fashion model and actress

Self-made cosmetics tycoon, Helena Rubenstein, was philosophical about money:

> *I can't help from making money, that is all.*
> New York Journal American, 1958

Money is the root of all good.

> Ayn Rand
> Writer and founder of
> the "Objectivism" philosophy

Olga Korbut, Russian gymnast who broke Olympic records in 1976, talks about money:

> *It's better to have a rich soul than to be rich.*
> People, July 19, 1976

For ten thousand dollars I'd endorse an opium pipe.

> Fanny Brice
> Comic, singer

Katharine Hepburn discusses money:

> *We've lost our wits about money. The lack of it is
> certainly most unfortunate, but who in the hell wants
> great piles of it? Many of my peers are fornicating on
> the screen for money, and that is ludicrous. I figure
> that I've made fifty times the amount of money I should
> have in my career, but the important thing is that I had
> fun.*

> People, October 11, 1976

*Nothing buys happiness, but money can certainly hire it for
short periods in expensive restaurants or careless weeks on
Austrian skis.*

> Irma Kurtz
> Writer
> 1973

*As a cousin of mine once said about money, money is always
there but the pockets change; it is not in the same pockets
after a change, and that is all there is to say about money.*

> Gertrude Stein
> Poet

*A private railroad car is not an acquired taste. One takes to it
immediately.*

> Mrs. August Belmont
> Victorian socialist leader
> *The Fabric of Memory*

I always remember the first script I wrote (for "The Goldbergs"). Jake came home for supper with a little ambitious bug in his brain. He wanted to go into business and he told this to Molly and Molly had some money she had put away anticipating just such a time and she gave it to him, and as they sat down to the dinner table he said to her, "Molly, darling, someday we'll be eating out of golden plates," and Molly turned to him and said, "Jake, darling, will it taste any better?" I always remember that.

Gertrude Berg
Actress and writer

Money is what you'd get on beautifully without if only other people weren't so crazy about it.

Margaret Case Harriman
Writer

We women don't care too much about getting our pictures on money as long as we can get our hands on it.

Ivy Baker Priest
United States Secretary of the Treasury
1954

Entertainer Vivian Reed, star of "Bubbling Brown Sugar" says:
I got a sense of being careful about money from my mother. Tomorrow isn't promised to us. This business (theatre) is crazy and you'd be a fool to think you'll be on top the rest of your life.

People, May 10, 1976

Louisa May Alcott, oppressed by the poverty resulting from her noted father's business ventures, wrote:
Resolved — to take fate by the throat and shake a living out of her.

Louisa May Alcott, 1832 - 1888
Journal

Louisa May Alcott

Elaine Markson

You're not really poor until you put water on the cornflakes.
　　　　　　　　Elaine Markson
　　　　　　　　Literary agent
　　　　　　　　(Jimmy Breslin's column,
　　　　　　　　New York Daily News, 1976)

Money speaks sense in a language all nations understand.
　　　　　　　　Aphra Behn, 1640 -1689
　　　　　　　　First professional English woman writer;
　　　　　　　　imprisoned for debt in mid-life

Organized charity is doing good for good-for-nothing people.
　　　　　　　　Elizabeth Barrett Browning, 1806 - 1861
　　　　　　　　Poet

Barbara Howar speaks of taxes:

> *My father said I'd be much less of a radical once I had*
> *something to lose, and I hate to agree with him, but it's*
> *true. I'd like to know what they're spending it on.*
>
> Barbara Howar
Writer and broadcaster

Barbara Hutton, between husbands, said:

> *Money alone can't bring you happiness, but money alone*
> *has not brought me unhappiness — I won't say my previous*
> *husbands thought only of my money, but it had a certain*
> *fascination for them.*
>
> Barbara Hutton
Heiress
1956

Is there some clue in the fact that I have never respected money?
"Money clutters my mind," I say in a charming, girlish voice.
"I am glad to give it to someone else to handle." Why, when I
work diligently and rarely shirk any other responsibilities, is
handling money too much of a responsibility? "Money is more
than paper. It is caring, concern — and sometimes love." The
answer suddenly comes in the midst of applying my morning
make-up. Not managing it is one of my devices to feel —
cared for.

Ethel Seldin-Schwartz
Writer
Diary of a Middle-Aged Divorce
MS, April, 1976

Money can bring many kinds of freedom. The freedom to feel
secure about yourself. The freedom to change what you can't
abide. The freedom to help those you love . . . and to help your-
self as well.

So please remember, when you take charge of your financial
future you also take charge of your life . . .

A $9.95 Texas Instruments calculator and a few dollars well

Maggie Tripp

invested in stocks and bonds can probably do more for a woman than greeting a man at the door in nothing but Saran wrap! Especially as time goes by . . .

Maggie Tripp
Feminist writer and lecturer
Speech in Dallas, Texas,
April, 1977

By law, public sentiment and religion from the time of Moses down to the present day, woman has never been thought of other than as a piece of property, to be disposed of at the will and pleasure of man. Women must be educated out of their unthinking acceptance of financial dependence on man into mental and economic independence. (Women must not) sell themselves — in marriage or out — for bread and shelter.

Susan B. Anthony, 1820 - 1906

The subject of inheritance in India is a strange one. While it is quite clear to my brothers that in a "joint" Hindu family, the boys inherit everything and in turn "take care" of their unmarried sisters and those of their married sisters who have not made lucrative matrimonial alliances, it is quite clear to me that all property must be equally divided (the law in this case can be made to swing in more than one direction). The "taking care" then becoming a matter of personal preference, flowing from brother to sister or sister to brother as need arises. We argue a lot. But I am the one who is uneasy and has nightmares about the hurt looks in my brothers' eyes as I question their traditional position. I wonder if they ever have nightmares about my uneasiness or are even aware of the unfairness.

Madhur Jaffrey
Indian actress and writer
MS, February, 1976

Madhur
Jaffrey

Chapter Seven

WHAT WOMEN SAY ABOUT MEN

Don't count on me for logic when it comes to men. I've had
a father, a husband, a son, friends, and lovers, and I still don't
have the foggiest idea what men are all about. The only solid
fact I cling to is that they are sure different from the rest of us.

The difference has been a dividing mechanism for me,
mentally separating the world into the "Women's Area," where
anything goes, and the "Men's Compound," where I'm not too
sure of the ground rules. But I *am* sure that somehow, some-
where, ground rules exist.

Movement women point out that my refusal to understand
the ground rules is because the rules are unbearably oppressive
to women — and I would prefer to float in the mists than confront *that.* It's partially true. The concept of women as the
support system for men nauseates me.

And I'm angry about the division in my head. It's Pavlov
and the dogs. Unthinking response. I'm trying to change, but
the old patterns are strong. I talk to other women and find they,
too, are having difficulty extending to their men the same
privileges that have always been given to their women friends.

De Beauvoir's phrase "the Other" comes to mind, juxta-
posed. Men have always been "the Other." Is it possible for
"the Others" to become One?

Here's what other women say about men . . .

Graffito from a wall in Chicago, 1971:
Yo' ain't the man yo' mamma wuz . . .

White knights are practically extinct.

Dee Dee Ahern and Betsey Bliss
The Economics of Being A Woman

Jane Howard, author of *A Different Woman,* speaks about men:
Several men I can think of are as capable, as smart, as funny,
as compassionate and as confused — as remarkable, you
might say — as most women.

Jane Howard
Life, Special Report on Women

The idea is for a woman to make her life as big, as challenging as
she can, and know that during that life there will be men who
will love her for what she is trying to be, just as there have always
been men who loved her for not trying to be anything at all.

Lee Grant, 1972

Women have served all these centuries as looking glasses
possessing the magic and delicious power of reflecting the
figure of man at twice its natural size.

Virginia Woolf
A Room of One's Own

Men who flatter women do not know them; men who abuse
them know them less.

Madame de Salm
American actress, born 1840

He's the kind of bore who's here today and here tomorrow . . .

Binnie Barnes
Actress

*If man is only a little lower than the angels, the angels should
reform.*

Mary W. Little

Explaining why "rabbit food" may be good for executives,
Dr. Aurelia Porter said:

*Middle-aged rabbits don't have a paunch, do have their
own teeth and haven't lost their romantic appeal.*

Dr. Aurelia Porter
Endocrinologist

I'm lookin' for a man to
Wash my clothes
Iron my shirts
Blow my nose
Sweep the floor
Wax the kitchen
While I sit playin' guitar
and bitchin . . .

Women's Alliance West
Virgo Rising (Record)
"Talking Want Ad"

July, 1973: When a New York City mugger attacked Beatrice
McCormack and a friend, she punched the man down, and then
sat on him until the police arrived. In a statement to the press,
Ms. McCormack said:

*When anyone . . . bothers you, you don't take it, you just
let 'em have it!*

Scratch a lover and find a foe.

Dorothy Parker

*I ask no favors for my sex. I surrender not our claim to equality.
All I ask of our brethren is that they will take their feet from*

*off our necks and permit us to stand upright in the ground which
God has designed us to occupy.*

Angelina Grimke
American feminist

*Women want mediocre men and men are working hard to be
as mediocre as possible.*

Dr. Margaret Mead
May 15, 1958

*Talk not to us of chivalry, that died long ago . . . a man in love
will jump to pick up a glove or bouquet for a silly girl of sixteen,
whilst at home he will permit his aged mother to carry pails of
water and armfuls of wood, or his wife to lug a twenty-pound
baby hour after hour, without ever offering to relieve her.*

Elizabeth Cady Stanton

*A male chauvinist pig is a man who thinks, or behaves as if he
thinks, that women are not as good as men. Or he may think
of us as equal in importance, but only as long as we keep to
women's work — that is, taking care of him, his house, his babies,
and his interests. He will call this separate-but-equal. Only somehow separate-but-equal never ends up being equal to those who
are separate.*

Dale Carlson
Girls Are Equal Too

Representative Millicent Fenwick, after having made a speech
proposing the ERA to the New Jersey State Assembly:
> *One of my colleagues rose and . . . said, "I just don't like
> this amendment; I've always thought of women as kissable
> and cuddly and smelling good!" It was the kind of thing
> you really don't believe. The only answer, of course, was,
> "That's the way I've always felt about men and I hope, for*

Margaret Mead

your sake, that you haven't been disappointed as often as
I have."

Jean Stafford
Vogue, June, 1975

I wonder why men can get serious at all. They have this delicate
long thing hanging outside their bodies, which goes up and down
by its own will. First of all, having it outside your body is
terribly dangerous. If I were a man I would have a fantastic
castration complex to the point that I wouldn't be able to do a
thing. Second, the inconsistency of it, like carrying a chance
time alarm or something. If I were a man I would always be
laughing at myself.

Yoko Ono
On Film No. 4, 1967

A woman without a man is like a fish without a bicycle.

Florynce Kennedy and/or Gloria Steinem

Mme. Jeanne Manon Roland, 1754 - 1793, was a French revolutionary whose salon was the headquarters for Republicans and
Girondists. After the fall of the Girondists she was arrested, tried
before the Revolutionary Tribunal and guillotined. Her husband,
who had escaped to Normandy, committed suicide when he
learned of her execution. She was recognized as a wit, and
widely quoted:
The more I see of men, the better I like dogs.

Today I pronounced a word which should never come out of a
lady's lips. It was that I called John a Impudent Bitch.

Marjorie Fleming
Journal, 1803 - 1811

... (he) drank the guts out of my soul like a vampire drinks blood.

Rona Barrett
Columnist

He is every other inch a gentleman . . .
>Rebecca West
>Novelist

A gentleman is a man who buys two of the same morning paper from the doorman of his favorite night club when he leaves with his girl.
>Marlene Dietrich

If a man is vain, flatter. If timid, flatter. If boastful, flatter. In all history, too much flattery never lost a gentleman.
>Kathryn Cravens
>*Pursuit of Gentlemen*

It has been wisely said that we cannot really love anybody at whom we never laugh.
>Agnes Repplier, 1855 - 1950
>American essayist

A kiss can be a comma, a question mark or an exclamation point. That's basic spelling that every woman ought to know.
>Mistinguette
>French entertainer
>Theatre Arts, December, 1955

Love lasts about seven years. That's how long it takes for the cells of the body to totally replace themselves.
>Francoise Sagan
>French novelist
>People, October 11, 1976

Jill Robinson, author of *Bed/Time/Story*, writing about the myth of romantic love:
>*For some reason it is assumed that: (A) it is the woman*

who is obsessed; and (B) the man is trapped. We seem to have forgotten that men fall in love, die, and faint of it. Some of the men writers have even written about it. Many men love to know where they are going to be that night, and marriage makes a comfortable solution, sort of a guarantee.

Vogue, June, 1975

When you love someone all your saved-up wishes start coming out.

Elizabeth Bowen
The Death of the Heart

Love, with very young people, is a heartless business. We drink at that age from thirst or to get drunk; it is only later in life that we occupy ourselves with the individuality of our wine.

Isak Dinesen
Seven Gothic Tales, 1934

It's not the men in my life, it's the life in my men.

Mae West

I shall not in this book speak much of my love affairs, but they were, nevertheless, an important part of my life. I was a great lover.

Carrie Nation
Temperance leader
Autobiography

What's wrong with (dating) younger men? They have less problems, less bitterness and more stamina.

Sylvia Miles
Actress

How do you know love is gone? If you said that you would be there at seven and you get there by nine, and he or she has not called the police yet — it's gone.

> Marlene Dietrich
> *Marlene Dietrich's ABC's,* 1961

Variety is the soul of pleasure.

> Aphra Behn, 1640 - 1689
> *The Rover*

Designer June Francis, Vice President of Jane Colby Sportwear, worrying about making a speech to her sales force:
> *. . . I have trouble speaking before an all-male audience. I think they see me as a sex object — and I certainly see all of them as sex objects, so, — so much for that . . . "*

Singer Mary Garden to Senator Chauncey Depew, when he asked what was holding up her decollete gown:
> *Your age, and my discretion.*

Lady Caroline Lamb, describing Lord Byron:
> *Mad, bad, and dangerous to know.*

Lascivious man to writer Jill Johnston:
> *I want your body.*

Jill Johnston:
> *You can have it when I'm through with it.*

Most people who were around New York City in the 1940's have fond memories of Minnie Guggenheimer and her Lewisohn Stadium Concerts. That the concerts, ostensibly a public event, were *hers* was indisputable. She would appear during the intermission, wave to the audience, and chirp "Hello, everybody," into the microphone.

And the audience would roar back, "Hello, Minnie."

Stories about her are legion:

. . . introducing Ezio Pinza, Minnie read her notes wrong and announced, "Ezio Pinza, bass." Correcting it rapidly she said, "Oh, dear, that can't be right. A bass is a kind of fish . . ."

. . . thanking an official of City College for the use of their Lewisohn Stadium, Minnie told the audience, "I don't know what I'd do without him." Then she looked him up and down and mused, "I don't know what I'd do with *him, either . . ."*

. . . bringing on a prominent political figure, she tossed aside her prepared introduction and confided gaily, "I can only tell you his Who's Who is six inches long . . ."

Grumbling is the death of love.

> Marlene Dietrich
> 1961

Love has been in perpetual strife with monogamy.

> Ellen Key
> Swedish writer

Love dies only when growth stops.

> Pearl S. Buck
> *To My Daughter With Love*

Security is when I've fallen very much in love with somebody extraordinary who loves me back.

> Shelley Winters
> Actress

Everything in the world is based on sex. Just because I haven't found a man I'm going to settle down with the rest of my life doesn't mean I'm going to swear off. I will be looking till I die.

I walk down the street. I think, mmm, that's not so bad. Wonder what that would be like? If I don't feel that way, I hate to mess my hair up.

> Barbara Howar
> Writer
> People, May 3, 1976

Oh, what a dear, ravishing thing is the beginning of an amour!

> Aphra Behn
> *Emperor of the Moon*

Cooking is like love. It should be entered into with abandon or not at all.

> Harriet Van Horne
> Columnist
> Vogue, October 15, 1956

I love food because it is my friend, one that doesn't leave town for the weekend. If I feel lonely, a salami sandwich is never too busy to spend time with me. If I feel mean or ugly, soup never complains. A man may walk out, a refrigerator, never.

> Betty-Jane Raphael
> Mademoiselle, July, 1976

Latins are tenderly enthusiastic. In Brazil they throw flowers at you. In Argentina they throw themselves at you.

> Marlene Dietrich
> Newsweek, August 24, 1959

When asked how she felt about having a male secretary, Margot J. Fox, Assistant to the Comptroller of the City of New York replied:

> *Terrific! I found I felt much less responsible for him than I've felt for my female secretaries.*

Man experiences the highest unfolding of his creative powers not through asceticism but through sexual happiness.

Mathilda von Kemnitz, born 1877
German writer

When I was seven years old, the priest who heard confessions at our school thought I was a boy, because I had to confess that I drew dirty pictures. When I whispered, "No, Father, I'm a girl," the silence from the other side of the confessional screen was profound. He finally settled for telling me to pray, more or less continually, to the Virgin Mary and — baffling to an active farm child — to interest myself in sports.

Karen Durbin
Writer
Mademoiselle, May, 1976

Save a boyfriend for a rainy day — and another, in case it doesn't rain.

Mae West

Women are always romantic-minded given half a chance. Many a woman must have sighed in her bed thinking, "Why didn't those wonderful fellows come my way?" My dear, your chance is now here. Earn a fortune, become the head of General Electric, become President, Vice President, take over Ethiopia, conquer the Nile, and you'll have all the splendid fellows you ever wanted. For the good ones go where the catches are.

Pamela Mason
New Woman, February, 1975

If you haven't had at least a slight poetic crack in the heart you have been cheated by nature. Because a broken heart is what makes life so wonderful five years later, when you see the guy in an elevator and he is fat and smoking a cigar and saying long-

*time-no-see. If he hadn't broken your heart, you couldn't have
that glorious feeling of relief!*

> Phyllis Battelle
> Journalist
> New York Journal American, June, 1962

*I'm the world's worst date. I hate them. There's such pressure
to show that you're funny, witty, you can get along with people
in restaurants . . . the last date I had, I was so nervous I ate four
desserts. At the end of the evening the guy said, "Gilda, you're
a good little eater." He told me he'd call and he never did.*

> Gilda Radner
> Comic
> Mademoiselle, May, 1976

*. . . Getting back to dating is not easy. Being in graduate school,
I do meet men, and yet it seems that dating is certainly a lot
different now from when I was in college the first time. In those
days, it was expected that if we looked pretty and played hard to
get, men would flock to our door. Now I find that half the
responsibility for reaching out and showing some interest is mine,
and unless I make this rather terrifying effort nothing much
happens.*

> Jan Fuller
> *Space: The Scrapbook of My Divorce*

*I belong to a generation of women who are doomed to stagger
forever down the thin line between our upbringing and our now
allowable, indeed heavily encouraged inclinations . . .
    What could happen if I drove into a gas station, gave the
mechanic a big smile, and said, "Hiya, good-lookin', wanta fuck?"
    Would it be any easier than saying, "Hello there, would you
like to go to the movies?" Eighteen-year-old women can do it
and their tongues don't turn black. My tongue would turn black.
Maybe I could put an ad in some discreet literary journal saying,*

"Ms. O'Reilly will be auditioning new lovers from two to four on Tuesdays."

Jane O'Reilly
Writer
MS, April, 1973

One more drink and I'll be under the host.

Dorothy Parker

It takes weeks of wanting and not-being-able-to-have to build up a good case of lust.

Jill Robinson
Vogue, June, 1975

I've given up on lovemaking. It's become a gymnastic exercise — and I've never been keen on sports. It gets on my nerves when I'm asked, "Did you have an orgasm?" The word depresses me. I am not a cello. I don't like to be played on. I like a little mystery . . . I'm an old fashioned woman — I have wide hips and a narrow mind.

Germaine Greer
British feminist, writer

Comic Ivy Bottini, speaking of masturbation:
You know you're going to bed with someone you like.

No woman is truly free to be anything until she is also free to be a lesbian.

Charlotte Bunch
Editor of Quest: a feminist quarterly

All women are lesbians except those who don't know it yet.

Jill Johnston

Germaine Greer

Peregrine Higgins

*I doubt the concept of sublimation. Work, when work goes well,
gets you turned on in every area. It has the same effect as a
good lay...*

Peregrine Higgins
Designer

*It occurs to me one day suddenly, a shameful and saddening
thought. I have never loved. I have wielded my affection like a
Japanese cleaver with blade so sharp it terrifies. I have asked
not for love but devotion. I have traded blind loyalty for a
porous, breathing affection that swells and rises and occasionally
is beaten down only to swell and rise again. It is the inevitable
beating down, the loss or apparent loss of love, no matter how
brief, that shatters me, and so I have opted for something safer,
a dense, heavy loaf which comes out of the oven looking the
same every day and which appears to be wholesome only because
it is predictable. My marriage, my affairs, all, all have come from
this sterile arrangement with life.*

> Colette Dowling
> *How To Love A Member
> of the Opposite Sex,*
> Coward, McCann and Geoghegan

Woman's virtue is man's greatest invention.

> Cornelia Otis Skinner
> *Paris '90*

*A girl (and perhaps the same thing applies to a boy) would find
life less broken apart after a misguided love affair if she could
feel that she had been sinful rather than a fool.*

> Phyllis McGinley
> *The Province of the Heart*

In seduction, the rapist bothers to buy a bottle of wine.

Andrea Dworkin
Woman-Hating

Submit to him!

Marabel Morgan
Total Woman

Question: How have most men had sex with you?
Answer: Badly.

The Hite Report

*First time you buy a house you see how pretty the paint is and
buy it. The second time you look to see if the basement has
termites. It's the same with men.*

Lupe Velez
Film star

All men are alike in the light.

Anonymous feminist
1976

Lorna Luft talking about living with a man:
*Listen, you wouldn't buy a pair of shoes without trying
them on for size, would you?*

*It has taken me a long time to realize when I say I don't trust
men what I really mean is that I don't trust myself with men.*

Terry Shultz
Mademoiselle, July, 1976

Freedom is not taking the guy home.

Gisella Heinemann
Writer

Andrea Dworkin

Chapter Eight

WHAT WOMEN SAY ABOUT MARRIAGE

I've been listening to women talk about marriage all my life.
It seems to me that those who have never been married are more
enthusiastic about it than those who have. And the many-times-
married view it as seasonal. True, there are occasional "true
love" liasons, but they are the exception, not the rule.

In my circle there is general agreement that no babies
should be without it. The family as the most efficient child-
rearing unit still holds sway. But there is equal talk about the
evils of raising kids in a loveless marriage; such fraud destroys
the integrity of all concerned.

I'm cheered by the lessening pressure on young girls to get
married. "Do something with yourself first" is the message now
— so you'll have good things to go on to when your kids start
school. It takes the "career" aspect out of marriage and puts it
back inside the girl.

All the children-oriented talk bypasses the nitty-gritty of
marriage: the vast amounts of hard work that go into making
a relationship work. Commitment, trust — all the lace-covered
words — represent, to many of us, the need to confront our
terrors and to learn to live with them.

Somebody (and I've been unable to track this one down)
once said that the real heros of our times are not the astronauts
and space explorers, they are the people who have good relationships. I agree.

Here's what other women say about marriage . . .

Speaking of her thirty-year marriage, Mary Stewart, author of *Touch Not the Cat*, says:

It was like suddenly coming into a harbor after a very rough and beastly sea.

People, September 6, 1976

Wedlock: The deep, deep peace of the double bed after the hurley-burley of the chaise longue.

Mrs. Patrick Campbell, 1867 - 1940
British actress

He came into my life as the warm wind of spring had awakened flowers, as the April showers awaken the earth. My love for him was an unchanging love, high and deep, free and faithful, strong as death. Each year I learned to love him more and more.

Anna Chennault
A Thousand Springs, 1962

When the wedding march sounds the resolute approach, the clock no longer ticks; it tolls the hour . . . the figures in the aisle are no longer individuals; they symbolize the human race.

Anne Morrow Lindbergh
Dearly Beloved

Clare Boothe Luce writing about her husband, Henry:

. . . for the truth of the matter is, women need to love and to be loved, for life without love is crippling at best, and meaningless at worst. It's just a pity that a woman is asked so often to sacrifice her personhood in order to fulfill her womanhood.

Only men who are of large spirit and who are really superior are, perhaps, capable of loving a woman enough to permit her to be altogether a person. My Harry was a man like that.

Letitia Baldridge
Of Diamonds and Diplomats,
Houghton Mifflin

Comic Phyllis Diller comments:
Never go to bed mad. Stay up and fight.

Actress Blanche Bates, discussing her short-lived marriage in 1896:
*At this period of my life I seem to have a fad for brief
engagements.*

*What happens when the wife piggybacks her dream and it does
come true? For fifteen or twenty years she has been living off
the vicarious fruits of her husband's slowly ripening success, very
often acting as his inspiration, intuiting for him how to treat the
people he works with, insulating him from the humdrum of how
to get the roast thawed in time for unexpected guests, and spar-
ing him the million and one details of feeling that have gone
into cultivating the children. The fruits of expectation may have
been fine to savor, but when it comes time for the awards to be
passed out, he is the one who walks to the podium to bask in
recognition. She is known only as Mrs. Brown, as in "Find
Mrs. Brown a chair," an uncomfortable appendage no one quite
knows what to do with.*

    *Coming into their forties, many women find themselves no
longer satisfied to be silent carriers of the dream that formerly
made them feel safe. "I feel this reemergence of competitiveness,"
the wife of one admired man explained. "I think the reason I'm
so shaky now is, I don't know what to do with it."*

Gail Sheehy
Passages, E.P. Dutton

*Women feel that if they don't go home at five o'clock and get
the socks washed and the dinner cooked, they will lose their
man. They are afraid to put the relationship to the test by
confronting the issue.*

    *When women ask for help they begin to work out better
relationships with the people they live with. Men are delighted
to be included. It gets them involved in something helpful. Most*

marriages get perfunctory as they go along. This starts something positive in the relationship.

> Maggie Tripp
> Lecturer and author

Data from a study on executive women points out the need for closer communication between working marriage partners:

The women . . . who work out their plans together with their husbands continue to have strong marriages. Those who make their decisions independently have had trouble . . .

> Dr. Anne Jardin and Dr. Margaret Henning

My life with Richard (Burton) certainly hasn't been a tragedy — we had the most gorgeous years together. Even our re-marriage, which turned out to be a disaster, was a marvelous lesson. Maybe I was just getting too old for him. I suppose when they reach a certain age some men are afraid to grow up. It seems the older men get, the younger their new wives get.

> Elizabeth Taylor
> London Daily Express, 1976

Actress Elizabeth Ashley, speaking about her past marriage:

Look, baby, I've lived a fabulous life. I kind of look at it like a car trip across the country — you remember the cities you passed through, but not much about them. George was one of those cities.

Everyone is a homemaker because everyone, men and women, contributes in some way to the development of a home.

> Jackie Mackay
> *Future Homemakers of America*

Elizabeth Taylor

Dale Evans

I think it would be harder for me if I weren't married to a writer. Writers are very boring to live with. I couldn't be as self-absorbed as I am.

> Joan Didion
> Writer
> People, July 26, 1976

Dale Evans, talking about her many years of marriage to Roy Rogers:
> *We've leaned on each other through the years and we've both leaned on God.*

> People, October 18, 1976

Ruth Graham telling how she copes with being the wife of evangelist Billy Graham:
> *(I) just pray for a thick skin and a tender heart.*

Muriel Humphrey, to her husband:
> *Hubert, to be eternal you don't have to be endless.*

If my husband would ever meet a woman on the street who looked like the women in his paintings, he would fall over in a dead faint.

> Mrs. Pablo Picasso
> Quote, 1955

I can never tell anyone how delightful it was to live by the side of a mind so fresh and original, so prodigal of its intellectual capital . . . it seems to me now that I am in danger of mental starvation.

> Elizabeth Cabot Cary Agassiz,
> written after her husband's death
> in 1873. She went on, in widow-
> hood, to become the first president
> of Radcliffe College.

I was not that I was against marriage, despite my initial unhappy experience. But . . . I picked a life that dealt with excitement, tragedy, mass calamities, human triumphs and human suffering. To throw my whole self into recording and attempting to understand these things, I needed an inner serenity as a kind of balance. This was something I could not have if I was torn apart for fear of hurting someone every time an assignment of this kind came up.

Margaret Bourke-White, 1904 - 1971
Photographer
Portrait of Myself

Producer Cheryl Crawford, at twenty-seven, speaking to novelist Edna Ferber:

Crawford: How does it feel to be an old maid?
Ferber: It's rather like drowning — not bad once you stop struggling.

I married for the first time at thirty-seven. I got the man I wanted. It could be construed as something of a miracle considering how old I was and how eligible he was . . .

But I don't think it's a miracle that I married my husband. I think I deserved him. For seventeen years I worked hard to become the kind of woman who might interest him. And when he finally walked into my life I was just worldly enough, relaxed enough, financially secure enough (for I also worked hard at my job) and adorned with enough glitter to attract him. He wouldn't have looked at me when I was twenty, and I wouldn't have known what to do with him.

Helen Gurley Brown
Sex and the New Single Girl

It is always incomprehensible to a man that a woman should ever refuse an offer of marriage.

Jane Austen

Helen Gurley Brown

Amelia Earhart, writing to her husband-to-be, on the morning
of their wedding, February 8, 1931:

*Dear G.P. — there are some things which should be writ.
Things we have talked over before — most of them.*

*You must know my reluctance to marry, my feeling
that I shatter thereby chances in work which mean so much
to me . . .*

*In our life together I shall not hold you to any medieval
code of faithfulness to me, nor shall I consider myself bound
to you similarly. If we can be honest I think the difficulties
which arise may best be avoided.*

*Please let us not interfere with each other's work or
play, not let the world see our private joys or disagreements.
In this connection I may have to keep some place where I
can go to be by myself now and then, for I cannot guarantee
to endure at all times the confinement of even an attractive
cage.*

*I must exact a cruel promise, and that is that you will
let me go in a year if we find no happiness together.*

I will try to do my best in every way.

A.E.

*The popular notion about marriage and love is that they are
synonymous, that they spring from the same motives and cover
the same human needs. Like most popular notions this also rests
not on actual facts but on superstition.*

*Marriage and love have nothing in common; they are as far
apart as the poles; are, in fact, antagonistic to each other. No
doubt some marriages have been the result of love . . . on the
other hand, it is utterly false that love results from marriage.*

Emma Goldman
Anarchist, free thinker
Marriage and Love, 1917

When asked about the problems of marriage, columnist Rona
Barrett said:

*The key is to let him think whatever he wants, and then
go at your own pace.*

Husbands are like fires. They go out when unattended.
> Zsa-Zsa Gabor

On the whole, I haven't found men unduly loathe to say,
"I love you." The real trick is to get them to say, "Will you
marry me?"
> Ilka Chase
> Writer
> This Week, February 5, 1956

Marrying a man is like buying something you've been admiring
for a long time in a shop window. You may love it when you
get it home, but it doesn't always go with everything else in the
house.
> Jean Kerr
> *The Snake Has All The Lines,*
> Doubleday

Husbands are awkward things to deal with; even keeping them
in hot water will not make them tender.
> Mary Buckley

How can one possibly eat ten thousand breakfasts with
the same man?
> Ann Bayer
> Writer

I married him for better and for worse but not for lunch.
> Mrs. Casey Stengel

1798: Mary Wollstonecraft (Shelley) to her first husband,
William Godwin:
> *I wish you, from my soul, to be riveted in my heart,*
> *but I do not desire to have you always to my elbow.*

Mae West

You should marry for sex or money and you're really lucky if you can get both.

Mae West

I don't give a damn about marriage, but I do care about honor.

Katharine Hepburn
People, October 11, 1976

It is better to be the widow of a hero than the wife of a coward.

Dolores Ibarruri (La Passionaria)
Speech, 1936

Marriage is as certain a bane to love as lending money is to friendship.

Aphra Behn
The Rover, 1674

Some day, some day men and women will rise, they will reach the mountain peak, they will meet big and strong and free, ready to receive, to partake, and to bask in the golden rays of love . . . If the world is ever to give birth to true companionship and one-ness, not marriage, but love will be the parent.

Emma Goldman
Marriage and Love, 1917

Being married was like an incurable illness. You have to chop it off to get well.

Christina Onassis

Pat Loud spotlighted the "Catch-22" feelings many American women have following the end of their marriages:

> *. . . The fact of the matter was that I felt like the failure, the shoddy, dumb, flat-chested broad who couldn't even hold on to her husband. The self-hatred hurt more than anything Bill had done.*

Marriage is to women a state of slavery.

> Lucy Stone
> American feminist

*Prostitution works two ways. When a woman sells herself,
either inside or out of marriage, she sells herself short. She gets
material things; some form of security. And when a man buys
a woman, either inside or out of marriage he has sold out, too.
He only gets a small portion of her — the part he's paid for.
The unspoken agreement: much of each person is hidden, not
available to the purchaser.*

> Irene Haber-Myers
> Purser for one of the world's
> most experienced airlines

*I have never known my husband to approve any act of mine
which I myself valued.*

> Julia Ward Howe
> Composer of Battle Hymn
> of the Republic, 1862

*Although he doesn't know it, I have attended his funeral
several times. Each time I look* adorable *in my tight-fitting suit
and Spanish lace veil. And, each time, after a decent period has
elapsed, I have remarried a very rich man and become famous
for the ethereal look on my beautiful pale face.*

> Christine Billson
> *You Can Touch Me,* 1961

Julia Ward Howe

Chapter Nine

WHAT WOMEN SAY ABOUT POLITICS

A few years ago my father and I were reminiscing about our
early home life, and I mentioned the O'Malleys, the one family
in our neighborhood we were all told to avoid. We weren't to
play with the O'Malley kids, they weren't to set foot in our
yards. "Religious differences were so crucial in those days,"
I said to Pa. "Nonsense," he answered, "Religion had nothing
to do with it. They were Democrats, you know."

I began my political career early on, wearing an Alf Landon
sunflower to grammar school. It would have been odd not to.
My school was in Westchester County, a hotbed of Republican-
ism, if one can use those words together. All the other kids
wore Landon buttons too.

Four years later Wendell Willkie was running and we were
old enough to help get out the vote. We loved political work.
It was so exciting, the fact that our candidates never seemed
to win anything disturbed no one. After all, we were playing
the game.

Eventually I left the Grand Old Party, to free-float among
the activists where I learned about political action. I believe such
action is the only sensible route for the women's movement.
For the majority of the nation to have such a minute voice in
government is intolerable. Our representation must be changed
and our collective impact on male legislators must be sharpened.
Each of us must work in her own way; the important thing is
to *Do It.*

Here's what other women say about politics . . .

Inscribed on the pedestal of the Statue of Liberty in New York Harbor, 1886:

Give me your tired, your poor, your huddled masses yearning to breathe free the wretched refuse of your teeming shore, send these, the homeless, tempest-tossed, to me:

I lift my lamp beside the golden door.

Not like the brazen giant of Greek fame, with conquering limbs astride from land to land; Here at our sea-washed, sunset gates shall stand a mighty woman with a torch, whose flame is the imprisoned light, and her name

Mother of exiles.

Emma Lazarus
Poet

In 1970, Bella Abzug, speaking to the New York City Commission on Human Rights, outlined the position of women in political parties. She could have been speaking today . . .

. . . yes, our political skills are now very highly valued. We are allowed to do most of the drudgery and the dirty work and the detail work of politics. I would venture to say that there is no political party in the U.S. that could survive were it not for the fact that the women are holding up those structures on their backs. But, for the most part, women are still excluded from the political power they create. Women are a majority of the population. They are also a majority in every social and ethnic group. But they are almost invisible in government.

Men, their rights and nothing more, women, their rights and nothing less.

Susan B. Anthony

I became a feminist as an alternative to becoming a masochist.

Sally Kempton
Esquire, 1970

Bella Abzug

Abigail Adams

I am more and more convinced that man is a dangerous creature;
and that power, whether vested in many or a few, is ever grasping,
and like the grave, cries, "Give, give!"

Abigail Adams
in a letter to John Adams, 1775

American Feminist Ann Scott told this anecdote about herself
in 1973 . . .

One night the phone rang when I was sound asleep. I sort
of swam to the surface. A woman said, "How are things
going on the ERA?" So I immediately went into my rap
like somebody had pushed a button, and we talked back
and forth for about ten minutes. Finally, she said in a
peculiar voice, "Do you know who this is?" I said, "No,
I'm sorry, but I have to confess that I don't." She said,
"It's your mother."

MS, July, 1973

Political action became a part of the women's movement from
the beginning of N.O.W. Here's Florynce Kennedy, advising
participants:

You've got to rattle your cage door. You've got to let them
know that you're in there, and that you want out. Make
noise. Cause trouble. You may not win right away, but
you'll sure have a lot more fun.

Mabel Vernon, at eighty-nine, reminiscing about the women's
suffrage movement:

Although suffrage was quite generally accepted by educated
and thoughtful women, my own family didn't understand
it when I was arrested. My mother came to Washington
right away to see if there was anything she could do for me
in jail.

When good people in any country cease their vigilance and struggle, then evil men prevail.

Pearl S. Buck

If you can't get along with your lover you can get out of bed. But what do you do when your country's fucking you over?

Nancy Mann
New England Free Press

Mary Harris Jones, known as Mother Jones, involved herself in the labor movement following the death of her husband in 1867. The miners were her cause, and she fought for them, in and out of jail, for the rest of her life. When a judge in West Virginia said to her, "It seems to me that it would have been better far . . . to follow the lines and path which the Almighty Being intended for her sex to pursue . . . the true sphere of womanhood, " Mother Jones called him a scab.

Here's Mother Jones' advice to the women union organizers:

No matter what your fight, don't be ladylike.

Commenting on a surprise protest march around the White House, COYOTE (the largest U.S. prostitute's organization) founder, Margo St. James said:

It's been very successful. The politicians have had our tits in the wringer for years, now it's time to put their nuts in the cracker.

MS, September, 1976

Without fanaticism one cannot accomplish anything.

Evita Peron
1951

Betty Williams, organizer of the women's peace movement in Northern Ireland:

Those children — their deaths burst a dam inside me. It wasn't that God whispered in my ear or anything daft like that, but He told me to get off my butt and do something about this senseless and useless loss of life. The violence must be stopped. If I thought my own son would take up a gun to kill, I would give him a cyanide pill. I would destroy what I gave birth to if he tried to take away the life of another.

People, September 13, 1976

There is a mercy which is weakness, and even treason against the common good.

George Eliot (Mary Ann Evans)
Romola

I am not willing, now or in the future, to bring bad trouble to people who, in my past association with them, were completely innocent of any talk or any action that was disloyal or subversive . . . I cannot and will not cut my conscience to fit this year's fashion, even though I long ago came to the conclusion that I was not a political person and could have no comfortable place in any political group.

Lillian Hellman
Letter to Committee on
Un-American Activities
Scoundrel Time,
Little, Brown, 1952

Freedom for supporters of the government only, for the members of one party only — no matter how big its membership may be — is no freedom at all. Freedom is always freedom for the man who thinks differently.

Rosa Luxemburg, 1880 - 1919
German socialist

Golda Meir, addressing the U.N. General Assembly on the Soviet action in Hungary, 1956:

My delegation cannot refrain from speaking on this question. We have had such an intimate knowledge of boxcars and of deportations to unknown destinations that we cannot be silent.

A young Princess Margaret describing a public reception attended by royalty:

It was the usual "zoo tea." You know, we eat — the others watch.

Patriotism is not enough. I must have no hatred or bitterness toward anyone.

> Edith Cavell
> Nurse
> to the Rev. Mr. Garan, the night
> before her execution as a spy
> by the Germans, World War I.

The feeble tremble before opinion, the foolish defy it, the wise judge it, the skillful direct it.

> Mme. Jeanne Roland
> French girondist,
> 1754 - guillotined 1793

Conversation between Simone Weil and Simone de Beauvoir:

SW: The only important thing in the world is to mount a revolution that would give food to everyone.

SDB: ... the real problem is finding a meaning for human existence.

SW: Obviously, you've never been hungry.

Golda Meir

Gloria Steinem

It is better to die on your feet than to live on your knees.
> Dolores Ibarruri (La Passionaria)
> from a speech given
> in September, 1936

Justice is better than Chivalry if we cannot have both.
> Alice Stone Blackwell
> American feminist,
> daughter of Lucy Stone

It's not that women are less corruptible than men are, it's that women have had less chance to become corrupt.
> Gloria Steinem
> from a speech to the N.Y.C. Chapter,
> National Home Fashions League,
> early 70's

Let them eat cake.
> Marie Antoinette

Never retract, never explain, never apologize — get the thing done and let them howl.
> Nellie McClung
> First woman member,
> Canadian Broadcasting System,
> Board of Directors

Democrats think of government as an art form. They practice it, relish it; they're schooled in it. For them, it's a life's work. The Republicans think of government as a charity. They have a Junior League attitude: "I will give four years of my time." You never feel they enjoy it.
> Liz Carpenter
> Washington political figure
> People, December 6, 1976

Shirley MacLaine, speaking about President John F. Kennedy:

I'd rather have a President who was screwing women than screwing the country.

People, May 10, 1976

New Jersey Representative Millicent H. Fenwick commenting on her party's situation:

It's restful . . . we don't struggle over chairmanships. We never get knocked out because we're never in.

Eleanor Roosevelt, giving advice to the wives of political campaigners, 1962:

Always be on time. Do as little talking as humanly possible. Remember to lean back in the parade car so everybody can see the President. Be sure not to get too fat, because you'll have to sit three in the back seat.

Make policy, not coffee.

Motto of the Women's Political Caucus

Powerlessness is more corrupting than power. I hope power will change women and give them a sense of worth so they can fight the establishment and not each other.

Florynce Kennedy
Feminist lawyer

I long to hear that you have declared an independence. And in the new code of laws which I suppose it will be necessary for you to make, I desire you would remember the ladies, and be more generous and favorable to them than your ancestors . . . if particular care and attention is not paid to the ladies, we are determined to foment a rebellion and will not hold ourselves bound by any laws in which we have no voice or representation.

Abigail Adams
in a letter to John Adams, 1774

I believe we will have better government in our countries when men and women discuss public issues together and make their decisions on the basis of their differing areas of experience and their common concern for the welfare of their families and their world . . . too often the great decisions are originated and given form in bodies made up wholly of men, or so completely dominated by them that whatever of special value women have to offer is shunted aside without expression.

Eleanor Roosevelt
Address to the United Nations
General Assembly, 1952

Dr. Dixie Lee Ray, past Chairman of the U.S. Atomic Energy Commission, surprised the Establishment when she ran and won the Washington Democratic gubernatorial primary. In her campaign speeches she stressed:

I don't believe in a government elite. Power is insidious. It cannot be held too long by any one person.

Opponents of women's suffrage often enlisted regional stereotypes to bolster their arguments. Alabama suffragette Pattie Ruffner Jacobs, 1875 - 1935, answered arguments about the myths of "Southern Ladies" as follows:

The pedestal platitude appeals less and less to the intelligence of southern women, who are learning in increasing numbers that the assertion that they are too good, too noble, too pure to vote in reality brands them as incompetents.

Lynn Sherr and Jurate Kazickas
The American Women's Gazetteer

Francoise Giroud writes of the Women's Revolution:

. . . When will it take place? And will it take place? . . . will people search for responsibility? . . . I'm talking about the whole female population, that part of the human race referred to as "women." Aren't they going to be paralyzed with fear — which you can be sure will be

played upon — that they might lose their femininity? As though femininity is something you can lose the way you lose your pocketbook: hmm, where in the world did I put my femininity?

> Francoise Giroud
> First French Secretary of State
> for the Condition of Women
> *I Give You My Word,*
> Houghton Mifflin

One of the things I have always said about the man-woman relationship is that I don't want anybody to walk ahead of me and I don't want anybody to walk behind me. I want a man who will walk along beside me. And that's how I feel about equal rights.

> Cicely Tyson
> Actress
> Report of the National Commission
> on the Observance of
> International Women's Year, 1976

The whole flavor and quality of the American representative government turn to ashes on the tongue if one regards the government as simply an inferior and second-rate sort of corporation.

> Margaret Halsey
> *The Folks at Home*

We cannot turn the clock back to unmake the conditions which have given rise to twentieth century inherited prejudices, but we can refuse to accept the false notion that hate or fear of each other is an inevitable trait of human nature.

> Mildred H. McAfee
> Head of the Woman's
> Army Corps, World War II,
> Dean of Wellesley

All right, so we don't buy war as a concept. It's worse — we
buy it in reality . . . on April 15 we all sent in our tax dollars.
"Here," we said to our administration, "spend it wisely for me."
But we didn't give them a marketing list. And here we go again.
Sixty-five cents out of every dollar for every war — past, present
and future . . . Why? Because there are profits to be made on
Pentagon product.

Bess Myerson
Mother's Day Address, 1970

Once in cabinet we had to deal with the fact that there had
been an outbreak of assaults on women at night. One minister
. . . suggested a curfew; women should stay at home after dark.
I said, "But it's the men who are attacking the women. If
there's to be a curfew, let the men stay at home, not the women."

Golda Meir
Notes From the Third Year,
1971

When an Italian talks with an American he's inclined to feel a
twinge of inferiority. America is rich and strong. Italy is poor.
But when he talks to me, he's more at ease. I still represent a
big, strong nation but I am a woman — and he's a man.

Clare Booth Luce
U.S. Ambassador to Italy, 1954

We don't want to be the same as men, merely equal
as human beings.

Margaret Heckler
Congresswoman
Report of the National Commission on the
Observance of International Women's Year

Feminist Alice Stone Blackwell, when confronted with sneers
that women's suffrage had not brought the millenium, replied:
   There is a great deal of human nature in women.

*Women have one advantage over men (as union organizers) —
their egos aren't so involved. They can compromise to get what
they want instead of forcing a showdown all the time.*
                    Dolores Huerta
                    Vice President, United Farm Workers

*What a minority group wants is not the right to have geniuses
among them, but the right to have fools and scoundrels without
being condemned as a group.*
                    Agnes Elizabeth Benedict

*Women who want equality must be prepared to give it and
believe in it, and in order to do that it is not enough to state
that you are as good as any man, but also it must be stated
that he is as good as you and both will be humans together.*
                    Anne Roiphe
                    New York Magazine, 1977

*The main problem is to liberate the males. Every man I know
is a chauvinist, and none of them is happy about it. We're getting to the point where it won't be okay for* anybody *to cry.
If a woman cries, the feminists get her. If you're a man and you
cry, the rednecks get you. I want women to be liberated and
still be able to have a nice ass and shake it.*
                    Shirley MacLaine
                    People, May 10, 1976

The only question left to be settled now is: are women persons?
                    Susan B. Anthony

Shirley MacLaine

Chapter Ten

WHAT WOMEN SAY ABOUT RELIGION

Women have been quite silent about religion, which is not too surprising considering what the major religions have been saying about women all these centuries. Perhaps those who became involved did so because it was the only game in town; the logical belief in an "Almighty Being" spilled over to include the male-appointed interpreters of "His" (male) doctrines.

Belief delineated women. The "good" woman was also the devout woman no matter who or where she was. But she did her good works outside the sanctuary, skirting around the hierarchy that denied her equal participation. One wonders what results might have been achieved if she had been allowed to work from within.

Now the news media is full of controversy over women's demands to share all the roles and enact all the rituals. Female priests are appointed; services are boycotted. The Bible itself is being re-edited, to screen out masculine expressions not in the original, but introduced by early translators.

Is there any woman who, in some secret part of her, doesn't whisper, "It's about time?"

Here's what other women say about religion . . .

*All that is necessary to make this world a better place to live in
is to love — to love as Christ loved, as Buddha loved.*

Isadora Duncan
My Life, 1925

Superstition is but the fear of belief; religion is the confidence.

Marguerite Power, 1789 - 1849
Countess of Blessington
Irish woman of letters

(Sarah) Margaret Fuller, 1810 - 1850, was a Massachusetts born
writer, editor and social reformer. From 1839 to 1844 she conducted "conversations" with a group of Boston women as a means
of general cultural education, a forerunner of today's consciousness
raising groups. She wrote of religion:

*Women could take part in the processions, the songs, the
dances of old religions; no one fancied their delicacy was
impaired by appearing in public for such a cause.*

*One who has had a unique experience with prayer has a right to
withhold it from others.*

Madame Chiang Kai-shek
1955

God forgives those who invent what they need.

Lillian Hellman
The Little Foxes

*The Bible and Church have been the greatest stumbling blocks
in the way of women's emancipation.*

Elizabeth Cady Stanton
1896

Elizabeth Cady Stanton

*We send missionaries to China so the Chinese can get to heaven,
but we won't let them into our country.*

Pearl S. Buck

*. . . I hope I will be religious again, but as for regaining my
character, I despair.*

Marjorie Fleming, 1803 - 1811
Journal

Elena Petrovna Blavastsky, 1831 - 1891, was married at seventeen,
left her husband shortly after and journeyed to India and Tibet
where she became interested in spiritualism and the occult. She
is recognized as the founder of Theosophy, a philosophic doctrine
investigating the mysteries of nature and religion. From her
writings:

> *The Christians were the first to make the existence of Satan
> a dogma of the Church. What is the use in a Pope if there
> is no devil?*
> *. . . There has never been a religion in the annals of
> the world with such a bloody record as Christianity.*

*If God wanted women to be sex symbols he wouldn't have made
Mary a virgin.*

Patti Harrison & Robin Tyler
Feminist comedy team

To be a Jew is a destiny.

Vicki Baum
And Life Goes On

*People think we Christian Scientists do not approve of doctors.
That is just not true. I adore Marcus Welby. Some of my best*

*friends are doctors. We have them to our house for dinner all
the time. There isn't anything I wouldn't do for doctors . . .
except get sick!*

> Carol Channing
> Entertainer
> Speech at Bennington College, June, 1975

*Faith and doubt both are needed — not as antagonists but
working side by side — to take us around the unknown curve.*

> Lillian Smith
> *The Journey,* 1954

Margaret Harris, conductor, composer, pianist, ex-child prodigy
who gave her first piano recital at age three speaks about religion:

> *My mother was a very religious person, and I was taught
> that the talent I had was loaned to me while I'm on earth,
> that it was passing through me to others. That while I'm
> here I should use it to the best of my ability and it would
> not die with me, but be passed on like a torch in the
> Olympics. It may sound strange, but that's what I believe.*

> Suzanne Seed
> *Saturday's Children,* Bantam

Betty Robbins, a Long Island housewife, became the first woman
cantor in Jewish history. News summaries of the event, August 15,
1955, quote her:

> *I sing what is in my heart. My only thought now is to sing
> as I have never sung before.*

*I feel no need for any other faith than my faith in human beings.
Like Confuscius of old, I am so absorbed in the wonders of earth
and the life upon it that I cannot think of heaven and the angels.*

> Pearl S. Buck
> American novelist, 1950

Barbara Howar

The most important thing about me is that I am a Catholic.
It's a superstructure within which you can work, like the sonnet.
I need that. A good director tells the actors where to move
exactly; then they are free to act. *I'm grateful for that disci-*
pline, and I've never had a crisis of conscience.

Jean Kerr
Playwright and humorist

I'm a practicing nothing. I have strong rapport with the Lord.
When I run out of money, when I'm scared, when a plane is
landing or when something is wrong with the children, then I
make great bargains, "Get me out of this one, sweet Jesus, and
I'll never pull it again."

Barbara Howar
Writer
People, May 3, 1976

Chapter Eleven

WHAT WOMEN SAY ABOUT THEIR PERSONAL PHILOSOPHIES

The past two decades have seen women turning their worlds
upside down. Some have dared themselves into changes, some
have had changes thrust on them when they were pushed out
of their nests. The changelings often have a bravery to them
and an underlying impudence that allows them to say: all or
nothing.

Not everyone has been involved in dramatic new beginnings.
But even the most complacent among us must admit that civilization is edging around to where it is easier and better to be a
woman than ever before.

Risk seems to run through women's philosophies: risk
with integrity, risk to grow, risk because there isn't much to lose.
This is not surprising to me. Risk taking demands a flexibility
that is built into our concept of women's roles. Men specialize;
women can do everything.

Each of us has a certain magic charm that sees us through.
Sometimes it's a catch phrase, sometimes an attitude that had no
words attached to it. Whatever the guise, we slip it out and
fondle it when the going gets rough.

Here's what other women say about their personal
philosophies . . .

In addition to her other activities, Eleanor Roosevelt wrote articles, letters and columns addressing herself to the interests and problems of women. Recurrent themes through many of these were:

No one can make you feel inferior without your consent.

Life was meant to be lived, and curiosity must be kept alive. One must never, for whatever reason, turn his back on life.

People are more fun than anybody.

> Dorothy Parker

You do have to say "no" to the old ways before you can begin to find the new "yes" you need.

> Betty Friedan
> Epilogue, *The Feminine Mystique*

There I saw it: every woman's life is a series of exorcisms from the spells of different oppressors: nurses, lovers, husbands, juries, parents, children, myths of the good life, the most tyrannical despots can be the ones who love us the most.

> Francine du Plessix Gray
> *Lovers and Tyrants*

I have not ceased being fearful, but I have ceased to let fear control me. I have accepted fear as a part of life — specifically the fear of change, the fear of the unknown; and I have gone ahead despite the pounding in the heart that says: turn back, turn back, you'll die if you venture too far.

> Erica Jong
> Poet and writer

Risk! Risk anything! Care no more for the opinions of others, for those voices. Do the hardest thing on earth for you. Act for yourself. Face the truth.

> Katherine Mansfield
> Journals, 1927

Eleanor Roosevelt

Jennie Grossinger

Amelia Earhart, when asked why she took such risks, said:
   I want to do it because I want to do it. Women must try
   to do things as men have tried. When they fail, their failure
   must be but a challenge to others.

Progress is an alarm clock. Just when you're falling asleep,
it wakes you up.

Jennie Grossinger
Jennie and the Story of Grossinger's,
Grosset & Dunlap

Let me tell you something, dear, there are lots worse things in
this world than bad taste.

Diana Vreeland
Fashion authority

Suffering is also one of the ways of knowing you're alive.

Jessamyn West
American novelist

We only possess what we renounce.

Simone Weil
French political activist

If you look at life one way there is always cause for alarm.

Elizabeth Bowen
The Death of the Heart

Jane Addams, 1860 - 1935, became involved with the problems
of poverty on a trip to Europe following her graduation from
school. She returned to America to devote her life to activism
and social reform, establishing Hull House, the pioneer settlement
house in Chicago, and founding the Women's International League

for Peace and Freedom. In 1931, she was awarded the Nobel Peace Prize.

From her writings:

We slowly learn that life consists of processes, as well as results, and that failure may come quite as easily from ignoring the adequacy of one's methods as from selfish or ignoble aims.

Harriet Tubman, describing her decision to try to escape from slavery:

I had reasoned this out in my mind, there was two things I had a right to, liberty and death. If I could not have one, I would have the other, for no man should take me alive.

Security is mostly a superstition. It does not exist in nature, nor do the children of men as a whole experience it. Avoiding danger is no safer in the long run than outright exposure. Life is either a daring adventure, or nothing.

Helen Keller
The Open Door

A person who buries his head in the sand offers an engaging target.

Mabel A. Keenan

Iwo Jima, 1945: Photo journalist Dickie Chapelle talks about her work covering World War II:

It's not that I'm not afraid: Courage is not the absence of fear, it's the control of fear.

Some courage is closer to home. Brooklyn shopkeeper Millie Mandy speaks of her neighborhood:

I love it. It's my home. All right, so we need a little cleaning up of the addicts — I call them poor souls. I have never been scared here even when the neighborhood went down. I keep my door open and make the sign of the cross and keep on going.

Harriet Tubman

*In the turbulence of this anxious and active world many people
are leading uneventful, lonely lives. To them dreariness, not
disaster, is the enemy. They seldom realize that on their dead
fortunes, on their ability to withstand the fatigue of dull
repetitive work and on their courage in meeting constant small
adversities depend, in great measure, the happiness and prosperity
of the community as a whole . . . the upward course of a nation's
history is due in the long run to the soundness of heart of its
average men and women.*

Queen Elizabeth II
Christmas message
December, 1954

*Since my departure from Moscow I had often thought about
destiny . . . Go to meet destiny halfway and destiny will come
to your assistance.*

    . . . Freedom is a priceless gift. One has to pay dearly for it.

Svetlana Alliluyeva
Only One Year,
Harper & Row

*As for my part, I care not for death; for all men are mortal, and
though I be mortal, yet I have as good a courage answerable to
my place as ever my father had. I am your annointed Queen. I
will never be by violence constrained to do anything. I thank God
I am endued with such qualities that if I were turned out of the
realm in my petticoat, I were able to live in any place in
Christendom.*

Queen Elizabeth I, 1533 - 1603
The Practical Cognigator
Book of sixteenth century writings

*Some people are here on earth and never know what they wanted.
I call them unfinished business. I had a blueprint all my life from
childhood, and I knew exactly what I demanded of this world.
Now, some people may not demand of life as much as I did. But*

I wanted one thing that I thought belonged to me. I wanted the whole show. For me, that is living.

I don't say life was easy. For forty years, I wanted to jump out of windows. But I did feel I had the strength and the creative ability. There was never any doubt about that. No one could move me till I got what I wanted — on my terms, on earth. And I do. And it did take, maybe not the greatest mind, but it did take courage. And it did take despair. And the hardship gave me total freedom.

People have said to me, "Aren't you glad you were born?" Well, I had no choice. I didn't ask to be born. Just think of the burdens we have at birth. We're born to people. We have labels. And we have to carry them all our lives without our choice. It's a hell of a thing to be born, and if you're born, you're at least entitled to yourself.

> Louise Nevelson
> Artist
> (Diana MacKown
> *Dawns & Dusks)*

The executioner is, I believe, very expert and my neck is slender.
> Anne Boleyn, wife of Henry VIII

Shirley MacLaine, speaking of her reaction to her trip to China:
I realized that if what we call human nature can be changed, then absolutely anything *is possible. And from that moment, my life changed.*

There was a final paradox: After contact with a society that was communal, that smothered its creative culture, and saw art only as a way of serving the revolution, I began again to think about being an artist.

The intricacies of American politics suddenly bored me, and I no longer felt the need to travel to faraway places. I had my talent to think about now. I had spent too much time denying that talent, abusing it through misuse, being casual with it, or running from it. I had never really learned its limits. I had never really taken the talent I had on a long march.

After China I realized that the talent was there to be refurbished, to be nurtured, to be stretched to its furthest limits and made into something that would not only "serve the people" of my own country, but also serve myself. I was not a soldier or a philosopher or a politician; I could cure no disease, solve no economic problems or lead any revolutions. But, I could dance. I could sing. I could make people laugh. I could make people cry.

A week later, I walked into a dance studio for the first time in twenty years.

> Shirley MacLaine
> *You Can Get There From Here*,
> Norton, 1975

It seems that it is madder never to abandon oneself than often to be infatuated; better to walk wounded, a captive and a slave, than always to walk in armor."

> Margaret Fuller, 1844
> Writer, social activist

Even cowards can endure hardship; only the brave can endure suspense.

> Mignon McLaughlin
> *The Neurotic's Notebook*

What I am interested in doing is finding and expressing a new form of life. The Greeks lived. People do not live nowadays — they get about ten percent out of life.

> Isadora Duncan
> *My Life*

Following a precedent is an easy substitute for thinking.

> Ruth Smeltzer

October, 1957, socialite Elsa Maxwell, on television, discussing
life with Jack Paar:

> Paar: *Have you ever lost your composure, Elsa?*
>
> Maxwell: *Almost. I once ran out of my little panties!*
> *But you must keep your savoir-faire when you*
> *lose something. Keep on running!*
>
> Paar: *What did you do? Just kick them aside?*
>
> Maxwell: *Whatever you lose, never look back. Never think*
> *about it!*

If woman had no existence save in the fiction written by men,
one would imagine her a person of the utmost importance; very
various; heroic and mean; splendid and sordid; infinitely
beautiful and hideous in the extreme; as great as a man, some
think even greater.

Virginia Woolf
A Room Of One's Own, 1930

It would be nice if just once we could read a volume that began,
"When the first ancestor of the human race descended from the
trees, she *had not yet developed the mighty brain that was to*
distinquish her so sharply from all other species . . ."

Elaine Morgan
The Descent of Women

The only difference between a rut and a grave is their dimensions.

Ellen Glasgow, 1874 - 1945
American novelist

Prejudices, it is well known, are most difficult to eradicate from
the heart whose soil has never been loosened or fertilized by
education; they grow there, firm as weeds among stones.

Charlotte Bronte
Jane Eyre

Jane Addams

General notions are generally wrong.

Lady Mary Wortley Montagu
English woman of letters

Culture is what your butcher would have if he were a surgeon.

Mary Pettibone Poole
A Glass Eye At the Keyhole

*Change is an easy panacea. It takes character to stay in one place
and be happy.*

Elizabeth Dunn

Nothing in life is to be feared. It is only to be understood.

Marie Curie, 1867 - 1934

All change is not growth, as all movement is not forward.

Ellen Glasgow
Novelist

*Marriage, laws, the police, armies and navies are the marks of
human incompetence.*

Dora Russell
The Right to be Happy

In 1917, reformer Jane Addams was notified that she had been
expelled from the Daughters of the American Revolution because
she was a radical. Addams replied that she had supposed herself
to be a life member but had discovered that her membership
was only during good behavior.

The most exhausting thing in life is being insincere.

Anne Morrow Lindbergh

Mme. Anne Louise Germaine de Stael, 1766 - 1817, French writer, was exiled by Napoleon for ten years, returning to France after the fall of the Empire. An intellectual leader of her day, she was known for her wit:

> *To know all makes one tolerant.*

Regret is an appalling waste of energy; you can't build on it; it's only good for wallowing in.

Katherine Mansfield, 1888 - 1923
British short story writer

Falsehood is so easy, truth so difficult.

George Eliot, 1819 - 1880

In 1961, Louise Heath Leber was named New York State Mother of the Year. In one of her interviews she said:

> *There's always room for improvement, you know —*
> *it's the biggest room in the house.*

Lying increases the creative faculties, expands the ego, lessens the friction of social contacts. . . It is only in lies, wholeheartedly and bravely told, that human nature attains through words and speech the forebearance, the nobility, the romance, the idealism, that — being what it is — it falls so short of in fact and in deed.

Clare Boothe Luce
Writer and diplomat
Vanity Fair, 1931

In December 1973, Mademoiselle Magazine ran a section on "happiness." Writers Mary Cantwell and Amy Gross contributed:

> *An unbelievably large part of happiness/unhappiness is*
> *determined by semantics, e.g., the couple who used to be*

*childless is now "childfree." A nudist colony (tacky) is now
a "clothes-free resort" (not quite so tacky). So . . .
you are not dateless, you are datefree. Bald is dandruff
immune. In starvation circumstances, fatsos are better
equipped than skinnies. Having the flu means you get to
stay in bed and lose weight. Having a cold means you get
to stay in bed and eat. Splitting up with a suitor means you
have more time for your friends. Being fired means having
a chance to discover what you really want to do. Being
robbed will free you from being attached to possessions —
a significant karmic benefit.*

*Life is easier to take than you'd think; all that is necessary is
to accept the impossible, do without the indispensable, and bear
the intolerable.*

> Kathleen Norris
> American novelist

Knowledge is power, if you know it about the right person.

> Ethel Watts Mumford, 1878 - 1940
> American writer and playwright

Cynicism is an unpleasant way of saying the truth.

> Lillian Hellman, 1939
> *The Little Foxes*

Patience is a flatterer, sir — and an ass, sir.

> Aphra Behn, 1640 - 1689
> *The Feigned Courtesans, Act III*

*I have often observed that resignation is never so perfect as when
the blessing denied begins to lose somewhat of its value in our eyes.*

> Jane Austen

Madame de Maintenon, 1635 - 1719, French intellectual, mistress and then wife of King Louis XIV, was noted for her bon mots:
Nothing is more adroit than irreproachable conduct.

American born Nancy Langhorne Astor succeeded her husband, Lord William Waldorf Astor, in the House of Commons when he entered the House of Lords — becoming the first woman to sit in British Parliament. From her writings, 1930:
It isn't the common man at all who is important, it's the uncommon man.

It is not merely the trivial which clutters our lives but the important as well.

> Anne Morrow Lindbergh
> *Gift from the Sea*

A home is no home unless it contains food and fire for the mind as well as for the body.

> Margaret Fuller, 1810 - 1850
> Writer and critic

Life is my college. May I graduate well and earn some honors.

> Louisa May Alcott
> Journal

Hope is the thing with white feathers that perches in the soul.

> Emily Dickinson, 1830 - 1866
> American poet

Take off your hats to the past, but take off your coats to the future.

> Clare Boothe Luce

Katharine Hepburn

You can't change the music of your soul.

Katharine Hepburn
1972

Julia Child

A house is not a home.

> Polly Adler
> from the book by the same name

No vice is as bad as advice.

> Marie Dressler, 1873 - 1934
> Stage and film star

Civilization is a method of living, an attitude of equal respect for all men.

> Jane Addams
> Address in Honolulu, 1933

The world is round and the place which may seem like the end may also be only the beginning.

> Ivy Baker Priest
> U.S. Secretary of the Treasury, 1934

Letitia Baldridge recounts the advice one of her college professors, a woman, gave over cups of tea on Sunday afternoon:

> *. . . your main job in life, girls, is to be happy. And to be happy you must push to the farthest of your capabilities in all things, whether it's work or play, war or peace. Above all, keep your eyes open, look up as well as straight ahead, and for God's sake, know when to get off your tail!*
> > Letitia Baldridge
> > *Of Diamonds and Diplomats*

It's not true that life is one damn thing after another — it's one damn thing over and over.

> Edna St. Vincent Millay
> Poet
> Letter to a friend

Julia Child sums it all up:

> *It's hard to imagine a civilization without onions.*

Chapter Twelve

WHAT WOMEN SAY ABOUT OLD AGE

I realized I was becoming fascinated by age about ten years ago
when I found myself reading the obituary column with the same
"catch up on the old gang" feeling I have toward the society page.
It's no longer whose daughter is getting married, it's whose husband or parent has left us.

Coupled with the obituary column came an increased interest
in my own relatives — the older the better. When Aunt Lil celebrated her ninetieth birthday with a real bash, I was overjoyed.
My father's eighty-eighth delighted me as much as it did him. It's
reassuring to come from long-lived stock.

My mirror is not very reassuring. Depending on the light,
it all hangs out, or hangs down, rather. Now I understand the
accolades given to candle-lit rooms, vitamin supplements, and
getting a good night's sleep. Oddly enough, a good night's sleep
has become a pleasure instead of what you end up with when
there's nothing else to do.

As the visuals get more negative, I've begun to stockpile
wonderful activities, saving them for the days when I'll have
plenty of time. There will be hours to spend on music, courses
to take, crafts to learn, books to read, walks to take, conversations
to have. And best of all, time to sit and do nothing.

Here's what other women say about growing older . . .

Age is something that doesn't matter unless you're a cheese.
> Billie Burke
> Stage and motion picture actress;
> wife of Florenz Zeigfield

We grow neither better nor worse as we get old, but more like ourselves.
> May Lamberton Becker
> American critic and author

Time is a dressmaker specializing in alterations.
> Faith Baldwin
> Novelist
> *Face Toward the Spring*

Being old isn't nearly as bad as I thought it would be . . .
> Lena Horne
> Entertainer

When asked how she maintained her strenuous schedule at an advanced age, Minnie Guggenheimer answered,
> *It's easy. I just take six pills a day, recommended to me by six different friends, and a straight double Scotch before lunch and dinner.*

I'm fifty-six and still a Virgo . . .
> Liz Carpenter
> Press secretary to Lady Bird Johnson

Abolitionist Harriet Beecher Stowe published *Uncle Tom's Cabin* when she was forty. A few years after that she described herself:
> *I am a little bit of a woman, somewhat more than forty, about as thin and dry as a piece of snuff.*

Lena Horne

Josephine Baker

Paris in the 1920's and 30's was charmed by a young, black American woman who sang and danced with more verve than costume. Josephine Baker, legend before she was thirty, had this to say about aging (1966):

> *People have said to me, "You're getting older. How do you feel about that?" After all, my act is a young girl's game, but I don't even think about getting older. The trouble with most women is they get old in their heads. They think about it too much. They worry and worry and worry about losing their husbands to younger women, about being no longer useful — about all kinds of silly things. They shouldn't think about it. If they do they'll start wearing all kinds of funny clothes. They'll stop using good make-up and start doing all the wrong things that they think older people must do. Old age is something to be worn with dignity, knowing that you've lived and seen and experienced so many things that can be useful to the young.*
>
> Josephine Baker
> Monmouth Evergreen, 1970

Age is as meaningless as skin color.

> Diahann Carroll
> Singer and actress

Nature gives you the face you have at twenty; it is up to you to merit the face you have at fifty.

> Gabrielle (Coco) Chanel
> Fashion designer

Comic Phyllis Diller, speaking of face lifts:

> *When you can't get the eye-liner on because of the wrinkles, you know it's time.*
>
> People, October 11, 1976

. . . plastic surgery in itself has no power to make us girls adorable; that a firm character is much more important than a lifted face; that no person of any sex was ever more enticing than Winston Churchill as an old man, which didn't mean that one needed to have Churchillian wit, but only his interest in life as an unfrightening miracle.

Anita Loos
Kiss Hollywood Goodbye

'Tis a maxim with me to be young as long as one can; there is nothing can pay one for that invaluable ignorance which is the companion of youth; those sanguine groundless hopes, and that lively vanity, which make all the happiness of life. To my extreme mortification I grow wiser every day.

Lady Mary Wortley Montagu
Eighteenth century wit

Lady Mary Wortley Montagu

Golda Meir, asked if she was really going to retire, replied:
I'll give you my word I am. Listen, in May I'll be seventy-
five. I'm old. I'm exhausted. My health is fundamentally
sound, my heart is in good working order, but I can't
keep up this crazy pace forever. If you knew how often
I say to myself: to Hell with everything, to Hell with
everybody, I've done my share, let the others do theirs
now, enough, enough, enough!

Oriana Fallaci
MS, April, 1973

At forty-nine, Italian socialite Marella Agnelli talks about maturing:
Life gets better after thirty. Then it gets fantastically beau-
tiful. Guilt gets lost in time. I always thought it was my
American mother who transmitted guilt to me; one reason
I adored my husband's family is that they have this great
feeling that life is there to be enjoyed, not just as an axis
of duty and of expiation. But, after thirty, the guilt begins
to go.

Vogue, January, 1977

An archaeologist is the best husband a woman can have. The older
she gets the more interested he is in her.

Agatha Christie
Mystery writer

I've stopped telling friends that I would live to be one hundred . . .
now I say one hundred twenty-five; that way I'm sure to make
one hundred.

Georgia O'Keefe
Artist
At age eighty-nine

t important words in midlife are — Let Go. Let it
to you. Let it happen to your partner. Let the feelings.
Let the changes.

You can't take everything with you when you leave on the
midlife journey. You are moving away. Away from institutional
claims and other people's agenda. Away from external valuations
and accreditations, in search of an inner validation. You are moving out of roles and into the self. If I could give everyone a gift
for the send-off on this journey, it would be a tent. A tent for
tentativeness. The gift of portable roots.

To reach the clearing beyond, we must stay with the weight-
less journey through uncertainty. Whatever counterfeit safety we
hold from overinvestments in people and institutions must be
given up. The inner custodian must be unseated from the controls.
No foreign power can direct our journey from now on. It is for
each of us to find a course that is valid by our own reckoning. And
for each of us there is the opportunity to emerge reborn, authenti-
cally unique, with an enlarged capacity to love ourselves and
embrace others.

Gail Sheehy
Passages, Dutton

At my age and in my condition I'm going to do what I want —
I haven't got time for anything else.

Florynce Kennedy
Feminist lawyer

The whole world is absolutely brought up on lies. We are fed
on nothing but lies. We begin with lies and half our lives we
live with lies. Most human beings today waste some twenty-
five to thirty years of their lives before they break through
actual and conventional lies which surround them.

Isadora Duncan
Dancer
My Life

*I was always so busy living that I didn't have much time to
think about it. I learned about other things — my work — but
I don't remember having a mature thought on any subject
until I was about thirty years old. Sometimes I think everybody should be born thirty and start out from there. We can
learn, I am sure, until the day we die, and I for one am looking
forward to each day, each new thought.*
Mary Martin
My Heart Belongs, Morrow, 1976

When asked if she ever thinks about retiring completely, Helen
Hayes answered:
> *. . . every night about six o'clock. But then I get a good
> night's sleep and begin work the next day as usual.*
People, December 20, 1976

*I have a problem about being nearly sixty. I keep waking up
in the morning and thinking I'm thirty-one.*
Elizabeth Janeway
Writer
1973

Elizabeth Cady Stanton, writing to Susan B. Anthony:
> *. . . Courage, Susan, we will not reach our prime until
> we're fifty.*

Ethel Seldin-Schwartz writes of new beginnings in *Diary of a
Middle-Aged Divorce:*
> *I have started school. A young woman beside me asked
> what I wanted to be. I said I would like to become more
> of what I am already. She said she wished she had my ego.
> I told her it took time.*
MS, April, 1976

American folklore contains many anecdotes about aging.
Here's one ascribed to an old Appalachian mountain woman:

> *How did I git to be a hundred years old? Well, when I*
> *moves, I moves slow. When I sits, I sets loose. And*
> *when I worries, I goes to sleep.*

I keep myself in perfect shape. I get lots of exercise — in my
own way — and I walk every day. . . Knolls, you know, small
knolls, they're very good for walking. Build up your muscles,
going up and down the knolls.

Mae West
November, 1954, sixty-one years old

Speaking of her physical ailments, fifty-year-old author,
Mary Stewart, adds:

> *. . .all this makes me sound like a proper old wreck.*
> *The chassis may be, but the engine is fine.*

People, September 6, 1976

July 13, 1964, at her eightieth birthday party, Sophie Tucker
was asked to reveal her secret of achieving a long life.
She replied:

> *Keep breathing.*

There's no disgrace or shame in growing old. The problem is
how to deal with it. To be old is to have lived. We must
learn to cherish and value our experience instead of depreci-
ating it like some old model car. . . We should look at life and
age and growing old not with fear but with the hope of
fulfillment. We must work to create a more human society

*that maximizes the potential of everybody. That is authentic
maturity and authentic liberation.*

> Margaret Kuhn
> Founder of the Gray Panthers,
> national activist organization
> concerned with problems of
> the elderly

*Perhaps middle age is, or should be, a period of shedding
shells; the shell of ambition, the shell of material accumula-
tions and possessions, the shell of the ego.*

> Anne Morrow Lindbergh
> *Gift From the Sea*

After World War II, entertainer Josephine Baker was running
(and supporting) a village for children and animals in southern
France. Periodically she came out of retirement to do some
benefits for her village. In 1947, in one of the interviews to
publicize the benefits, she said:

> *I've lived several lives. I've enjoyed most of it. The
> people I've loved! Those who have loved me! The
> children! The animals! The songs! There's a heaven.
> Don't you doubt it. Did you know some of your dreams
> reflect the past and some the future. I dreamt I was
> floating nude down a stream on a lily pad and the stream
> was lined with thousands of cheering fans. That might
> be heaven — a look into the future. . . One must always
> be optimistic. Tomorrow will be better than today.
> Death will be better than life. That is, if there is such
> a thing as death. I'm not sure yet.*

> Josephine Baker
> Monmouth Evergreen, 1970

Two years later, in 1949, Helen Keller was speaking about life and death:

> *There's still so much I'd like to see, so much to learn. And death is just around the corner. Not that that worries me. On the contrary, it is no more than passing from one room into another. But there's a difference for me, you know. Because in that other room I shall be able to see.*

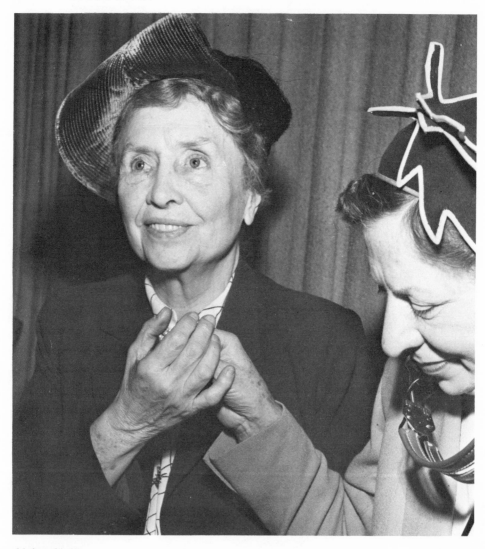

Helen Keller

index

INDEX